U.S. Tax.. Americans

The Traveling Expat's Guide to Living, Working, and
Staying Tax Compliant Abroad

Olivier Wagner, EA, CPA
Foreword by Gregory V. Diehl

IDENTITY
PUBLICATIONS

Identity Publications
www.IdentityPublications.com

To inquire about getting your own book or course produced, published, or promoted, email contact@identitypublications.com

U.S. Taxes for Worldly Americans by Olivier Wagner -- 1st ed.
ISBN-13: 978-1945884061 (Identity Publications)
ISBN-10: 1945884061

I want to thank all those who helped me on this journey:

Those who showed me that corporate America was not the best path for me. Robert Chayer and Jacinthe Marquis, who taught me many U.S. tax concepts and were always very patient and respectful with me.

John Richardson, who has supported my transition to a nomadic life. John has been with me through this journey and has helped me sustain my practice and discuss tax ideas.

Kasia Strzelczyk for her help at 1040 Abroad. Kasia has been an outstandingly reliable employee, ensuring that the business keeps turning no matter what misadventures I get up to around the world giving me valuable feedback on new ideas.

Gregory Diehl for overseeing the creation and promotion of this book. Gregory has been a longtime friend who I have watched blossom into a global citizen and entrepreneur (he only had one citizenship when I met him, and now has three).

Kevin Hoeltschi, Eric Z, Tyson Batino, Elisabeth Peltier, Chris Backe, Mariza Pavalama, Barbara Fernandez, David Hemmat, and Amna Shamim for giving me critical feedback on earlier versions of this book and encouraging me to keep going to bring my vision into real publication.

CONTENTS

FOREWORD

When I met Olivier Wagner at a digital nomad conference a few years ago in Bangkok, we were both already active global citizens. Each of us had the freedom to go where we wanted. We could maintain our income from anywhere in the world (so long as we could get online occasionally). We had adjusted fairly well to the complexities this lifestyle can carry, and were free to explore any opportunities the world could offer. The planet was our oyster, so to speak. We've come a long way since then though.

I have been traveling the world almost nonstop since age 18. While most people transition to nomadic or expatriate living after many years of following the conventional path, I have had the somewhat rare experience of spending my entire adult life exploring the world one country at a time. This path has taken me to more than 50 countries thus far and given me a profound new perspective on both myself and our planet. The experience has matured my mind and broadened my perspective in ways I don't believe anything else could have.

Though I grew professionally during my travels, collecting customers, registering companies, and opening bank accounts in various nations as I went, it would not be until I met Olivier that I would start to get serious about the tax obligation I was forced into as an American citizen by birth. I had enjoyed a comfortable upbringing in sunny San Diego. As a global nomad, I now took advantage of the ease of travel afforded to me as an American passport holder. But I rarely stopped to consider the seriousness of my home country's worldwide tax policy and how it could affect me.

As I traveled and worked online, I managed to do so in a mostly anonymous and "under the table" sort of way. I was always worried about coming out of the shadows and making too big of a name for myself. Not the least of my worries was becoming tax compliant. What if I filed something incorrectly? What if I didn't give the government enough information? What if I gave them too much? I had remained invisible to them this long. Why should I risk anything now by coming into the light?

Though I've now worked alongside some of the biggest names in "offshore" services, Olivier was the first person to clearly explain to me why it was important for me to get tax compliant. He made me see that avoiding my U.S. tax obligation would only get more complex and risky as time went on. As my earning capabilities increased, I would stand out more and more on the government's radar. He also showed me that if ever I planned to renounce my U.S. citizenship eventually, I would need to prepare now by getting caught up on at least the last five years of unfiled taxes.

Despite my unconventional work history and lifestyle, Olivier helped me get everything into the authorities on time while keeping my tax obligation as low as legally possible. I was finally, for the first time in my life, fully tax compliant. Getting to this point was an important milestone in my personal and professional development. As I continue to grow my influence, it's going to be even more vital that my financial affairs are in order and everything I do stays above board. Most importantly, I no longer have that nagging little worry in the back of my mind that if I ever get too successful or make too much noise in the world that everything I've built could come under attack by bureaucrats with busy fingers.

My situation is not entirely unique. I've befriended and worked with many U.S. citizens who have obtained multiple residencies and passports, started businesses in strategic locations, managed millions in nontraditional assets, retired on some tropical shore overseas, or even brought their children along with them as they sold their home and ventured around the world as a family. Each of them learned to branch out from the constraints of their home country to pursue their own version of an authentic lifestyle. They overcame the fear of the unknown to learn the rules of the new systems they were entering. Now they are each masters of those systems. You can do the same with whatever new systems lay before you: be that the United States tax system or any other.

A CHANGE IN MINDSET

Recently, I began chronicling the lessons this lifestyle has taught me in books and other online educational materials. That is why I was so glad to be able to help Olivier bring this book together into the finished version you are reading now. I realized he wanted to go beyond giving an overview of how to file your taxes from overseas. He wanted to introduce a new way of living to people who might, at first, be intimidated by all the little details they didn't understand. His goal is to open their minds to new ways of existing. Just as he helped me, his words here will broaden your mindset about how to live a worldlier existence.

Mindset determines everything in our lives. Your mindset is the beliefs you hold about how the world works. Mindset is what will show you your options for acting in the world. If a subject appears foreboding and complex (like the U.S. tax code often does), you will never explore the options it holds. If you don't know what options you have, you will never use them. Making foreign concepts feel familiar is vital to our continuing growth as individuals. This shift changes how you view both yourself and your place as part of the whole world - not just where you arbitrarily came from.

In spending the last decade living this life and mingling with the "experts" who dominate the professional industry, I've seen a lot of fear mongering and emotional bullying take place. The people who have a monopoly on uncommon and highly valuable information prefer to hold it over the heads of everyone who hasn't already discovered what they know. They scare ordinary people into taking massive actions they aren't necessarily ready for. That is how they maintain their social stature and financial livelihood.

If you poke around enough online about nomadic life, expatriation, or retirement overseas, you'll encounter a cacophony of voices all screaming at you to *"Move everything you own and everyone you love offshore before the government implodes and your dollars are worthless!"* Or they'll pressure you to follow in their footsteps and start living the "James Bond" lifestyle of martinis on white sand beaches, secret bank accounts, and homes on every continent. They are intimidating, overly posturing, and quite inaccessible for the average person. I'm sick to death of it and couldn't be happier that these once scarce resources are finally being made more available to the public through down-to-earth people like Olivier through his company 1040 Abroad.

Maybe you are just getting started on your journey away from where you grew up. Maybe travel and expatriation are still just ideas for you to play with until you understand all the steps involved. I believe that by sharing real stories and making these examples very true to life, Olivier's book will help you make significant progress in the direction of actually living the global lifestyle you desire. Although the information contained here is ostensibly about the intricacies of the United States tax system, I see it as a fundamental piece of a much larger puzzle about how to live a more fulfilling life beyond local limitations.

Think of this book as a partial guide to the much larger topic of expanding your identity beyond what the legal and cultural rule makers of your home nation told you was possible for your life. It may not cover the whole journey (no single book could), but it brings vital clarity to something many people consider to be the most obfuscating and offensive part of becoming a responsible world citizen. Just as Olivier's influence has brought a much-needed foundation to my once wild nomadic life, I'm quite sure that his book will do the same for you if you take his advice to heart in your unique circumstances.

To living life authentically anywhere in the world,
Gregory V. Diehl
January 2017
Author, *Travel As Transformation*
Founder, *Identity Publications*
www.GregoryDiehl.net

PREFACE

Are you a citizen of the United States who lives abroad? You might be an American who moved abroad, but who hasn't given up your original citizenship. Maybe you were born in the U.S., but have no real ties to it. Such "accidental Americans" are more common than you might think, and many of them don't even realize they are obligated to pay U.S. taxes. Maybe you've recently moved from the United States, and aren't sure how this affects your filing requirements. Have you established residency in another country? Do you still derive income from the US? Or in another country? All these factors will change your tax situation.

You could be a self-employed "digital nomad" who works from several different countries, moving wherever you want at your leisure. Despite such an unconventional way of making a living, you might still owe taxes to the U.S. If you don't file correctly, you could be missing out on important opportunities to reduce your tax burden legally. Or worse, you could end up with your own government revoking your passport and coming after you for the years of back taxes you may never even have known you owed them.

You may already know that the U.S. is one of only two countries in the world that taxes its people based on their citizenship, not on where they live or where their money comes from. If you make more than $10,350 per year (as of 2016) and are a U.S. Citizen, you still must file a return each year. Even if you can arrange things so that you legally owe nothing, you must still file. This can be especially problematic for those of you who have not filed U.S. taxes in a long time – or ever. How do you make sure Uncle Sam gets his due without suffering enormous penalties as you struggle to get compliant?

Maybe you have been told that you don't owe any U.S. taxes on money made overseas. This is true up to a certain amount, but only if you know how to take advantage of the proper avenues. Exclusions can cover the first $ 101,300 of earned income (as of 2016[1]), wages and self-employment income. To claim this exclusion, you must let the IRS know what's going on through the regular filing of your tax return. Combined with certain other tests and exemptions, it is possible for most people who work abroad to legally keep their taxes at $0.

How do you know if this is the right situation for you? How many days do you spend abroad each year? Do you have residency, bank accounts, or corporations in any other jurisdiction? How much money do you make as an

---

[1] The housing exclusion can further increase this amount.

individual or company entity? There is no one easy answer for every American living abroad, no matter what their circumstances. If you don't understand the full spectrum of possibilities which lay before you, you could end up paying a lot more than is necessary. Or worse, you could be considered tax non-compliant by your own government. You may be able to evade any negative repercussions for a while, but sooner or later you will have to face up to what you've been running from.

My work with 1040 Abroad (and my goal in writing this book) has not been to scare you into taking the action you have been avoiding. On the contrary, I wish to empower the people to live fuller lives and feel more confident in their actions by taking control of their unique tax situations. By reading the information contained here, you should get a much better grasp on exactly how the U.S. tax system uniquely affects Americans abroad, and you should be one step closer to getting the freedom of mind you desire.

If you like what you've read here, I encourage you to check out the wealth of articles on the 1040 Abroad blog for more valuable information like this. If you have any questions about what you've read here or want my help coming up with a plan for how to handle your U.S. taxes as an overseas American, I encourage you to email me directly at owagner@1040abroad.com.

Yours in freedom,
Olivier Wagner

INTRODUCTION

WHY THIS BOOK NEEDED TO BE WRITTEN

I grew up in France near Strasbourg, but always had dreams of living around the world. When I went to the U.S. in 2004, I studied the American tax system in Louisiana before moving to New York to work in corporate finance. In 2005, I finally received my U.S. green card and became a U.S. citizen in 2009. I had successfully climbed through the hurdles so many immigrants from all over the world strive to overcome, bringing into my life all the trials and benefits that a U.S. passport brings to its owner. I still retained my original French citizenship as well, so I was now a dual citizen of two of the most powerful and free-to-travel nations on earth.

With my new American wife, I stayed at my job in New York for five more years, until wanderlust came crawling back to me in 2011. That was when we decided to move to Canada, where I experienced life for the first time not just as an American citizen, but an American expatriate living abroad.

At this point in my life, the French government saw me as French, the American government saw me as American, and the Canadian government saw me as a Canadian resident. I was already living a very diversified life, mixing and merging international cultures and bureaucratic rules in ways that were completely unknown to me before. All that would seem small, though, in comparison to the major lifestyle overhaul I would experience just four years later when I decided to pack my bags and transition to a life of full-time nomadism around the world.

For the last few years now, I've embraced a life of much greater motion. I travel wherever either of my passports will allow me, whenever I want to. I've experienced life as an American and French expatriate in dozens of countries in almost every continent

While I know that I am not an American in the same way that someone who grew up in the U.S. is, as I didn't move there until I was an adult, I still think of myself as an American. In some ways, I have experienced more aspects of being American than most natural born citizens ever will. I've been a tourist, a foreign resident, an immigrant citizen, and now an expatriate living and working abroad. I've seen all sides of the spectrum: the good, the bad, and the many regulations it all entails. This is what ultimately lead me to the path of helping other Americans like myself in unconventional tax situations due to their worldwide lifestyles or identities.

There are three primary categories an American requiring special attention for their taxes might fall into.

EXPATRIATES

Expatriates are what most people think of when they picture an American who has left his home country. They live permanently or semi-permanently outside the U.S. in another country, but they have retained their American citizenship. They could be permanently retired or could be working long-term in a regular job in their new location. Either way, they aren't deriving any income from the U.S. itself. Expats pay taxes in the foreign country where they live, which allows them to use a Foreign Tax Credit when filing their returns back home. Because they already pay tax in a foreign country, they're more likely not to have to pay tax at all in the U.S. (but only if they file everything correctly).

PERPETUAL TRAVELERS

A true nomad is somebody who travels from place to place constantly, rarely staying in one place for more than a few weeks or months. Because of this transient lifestyle, they do not ever establish enough ties to any country to become a taxpayer there. They travel on tourist visas, or at most student visas. Most of them either have a nest egg of savings, are retired, or run an online business from wherever they go. This is a desirable path for Americans because it is the only way to make it so you never have to pay taxes because you never have to file a return anywhere else. But because these people still must file in America, even if they never set foot there during the year, I have to help them figure out how to set it all up to legally minimize their obligation.

ACCIDENTAL AMERICANS

An accidental American is someone who may not even realize for most of their life that they are, in fact, technically American citizens. Usually, they were born in the U.S., but they moved somewhere else when they were very young. Because America grants everyone born its soil citizenship by default, these people have been carrying this status with them for years and are blissfully unaware of the tax consequences it carries. It's a major legal and financial risk that a lot of people are subject to, but they aren't even aware of the danger. People who suspect they might fall into this category should talk to experts who can help them figure out their situation and what to do about their taxes.

The reason I help these kinds of people is because most U.S. tax preparers are only familiar with the tax laws for people who live and work domestically. It's quite a switch when you decide to take your life overseas in one form or another. The person you have been using for years to help you stay legal and above board might be totally out of his or her element when you make these lifestyle changes. Even if they are terrific in their specialization, they might not even realize there are endless new limitations and opportunities that now apply. Suddenly keeping your money in foreign bank accounts, running foreign corporations, and having residency or even citizenship somewhere else means there are now going to be rules that must be given special attention. There are a multitude of new forms to be aware of and strategies to take advantage of.

More people are renouncing their U.S. citizenship now than ever before. Each has their own reasons for doing this. Some are worried about the changing political landscape of today. Others pay attention to new rules and restrictions on freedom of travel, or (for better or worse) how the rest of the world views Americans. Mostly, they want to avoid all the complicated tax burdens that come with the territory of being a U.S. citizen. Part of my job is to educate them about how this process works and help them complete their renunciation through legal means if that is what is the best option for them. It's not necessarily difficult to get rid of your American citizenship, but it does warrant a lot of deep thought, planning, and a bit of money to pull off properly.

Many Americans living abroad have never even filed their taxes, or else haven't filed in many years. Some have been abroad so long that, aside from their passports and the occasional trip back home to see family, they have no real ties to the U.S. (not even a Social Security number). In their minds, they've long ago sworn off the idea of getting involved with U.S. taxes and would be completely financially unable to get caught up on them anyway.

Some of these people have been very lucky to coast under the radar this long without any consequences. It's very important that they get tax compliant as quickly as possible, and that they utilize every tool available to minimize their expenses at this time. There are very large consequences to continuing to ignore this. Yet, so many people don't pay any attention to it at all because it seems so overwhelming to consider. They may even take personal offense to having to pay anything at all. This kind of person will never get it all done on their own, and they need professional guidance to minimize their troubles.

Things are only getting more complicated for Americans living abroad as time goes on. Starting in 2015[2], a new law went into effect across the globe requiring foreign banks to identify which of their clients are American citizens. Foreign banks must report their name, address, and account balance to the IRS back home (although litigations between the Department of Justice and Swiss banks caused the trend to start in Switzerland as early as 2012 - one of my clients, a Swiss resident, saw 50% of his account balance frozen until he filed U.S. tax returns). It's called FATCA, and it stands for Foreign Account Tax Compliance Act. Additionally, anyone holding an equivalent balance of more than $10,000 in a foreign bank account must file an FBAR report. When the IRS receives this data, they will try to match that to the taxpayer on record as reported by the foreign banks

---

[2] The Foreign Account Tax Compliance Act (FATCA) bill was signed into law by President Obama on March 18, 2010. Its full implementation occurred in 2015. Who would have guessed that it would take five years to get every bank in the world to comply with local laws? Other aspects of the law went into effect earlier. For example, the creation of Form 8938 in 2011 was also an aspect of FATCA.

directly. The penalty for willfully failing to file an FBAR could be up to 50% of the account balance per year, giving serious caution to anyone interested in holding even some of their money offshore (or $10,000 per account if the failure to file was not willful, and possibly zero if the taxpayer had a reasonable cause).

Some Americans living abroad today know about the Foreign Earned Income Exclusion (FEIE), which allows them to exclude up to $101,300 (as of 2016) of foreign income from their taxable income. Nomads and expatriates who don't make a ton of money will typically use this to avoid paying taxes at all in the U.S., but only if they know how to claim things on their tax return correctly. One can claim the FEIE by being an actual resident of a foreign country (a "bona fide resident"). There's also a physical presence test for people who spend at least 330 days in any 12-month period outside the U.S. This is fine for those who have truly relocated outside the states, but what about others who still return frequently to visit friends and family, or split their time equally between multiple homes?

The information contained in these pages goes far beyond just filing tax returns. I wanted to give a more meaningful outlook on many aspects of international life, based on my own unique perspective having immigrated to and ultimately expatriating from the United States of America. I've lived the conventional stationary life, and I've hopped from place to place with great rapidity. This includes things of a technical nature, like foreign banking and incorporation. As well, I've included advice I've gathered after a lifetime of living as a multicultural expat

xviii · OLIVIER WAGNER

and citizen of the world to one extent or another. It includes the little necessities I've learned to appreciate that make my life easier, including mailbox services in the U.S. (where you can still have your mail sent locally, no matter where you are), Virtual Private Networks that allow you to access the internet in restricted countries, and even how to keep flight costs low when you travel.

I believe I'm able to guide others like me on many aspects of expatriating or living a more successful life abroad than you might already be. You can do all this and never have to risk your freedom or finances by staying 100% tax compliant as you go.

WHAT HAPPENS IF I DON'T FILE?

Many Americans have always been non-compliant. They have spent their whole adult lives outside the U.S. Others figure that since they won't be within U.S. borders, it would be impossible or impractical for the government to take any collection measures. Citizenship-based taxation dates back to the civil war, and in many cases such assumptions were correct. At the time, the IRS had little enforcement power outside the U.S. But as FATCA is now a reality, and all your personal information is digitized, this assumption is becoming less and less valid. Furthermore, the greater a person's income, assets, or foreign activities (such as having foreign corporations or foreign bank accounts), the more likely a person is to be noticed and the more they will have to lose. Both foreign corporations and foreign bank accounts come with filing requirements and potentially severe penalties for not meeting them. You'll learn all about these in the coming chapters. Before you decide to take this route, it's a good idea to fully understand the consequences you might encounter if you fail to file for long enough to get caught.

The first thing to understand is that anything you owe the U.S. that you don't pay while living overseas is subject to 3.25% interest. Though imprisonment is unlikely, you could face growing fines. Nonpayment of taxes can hurt both your finances and travel plans.

How do expatriates become compliant with the U.S. tax system? The 1040 isn't the only form you need to file. Many activities that seem benign can trigger specific filing requirements, and you may have to file other forms as well. The rules are the same for Americans living in the U.S., but Americans living abroad are much more likely to have participated in these "foreign" activities. They can bring about hefty fines (up to $10,000) if they're not turned in on time.

Depending on your situation, you may also need to know about Form 5471, Form 3520, and Form 8621. Form 5471 must be filed if you own more than 50% of the stock of a foreign corporation (or in some cases just 10%). Constructive ownership rules apply. So, for reporting purposes, you could be considered to be owning shares which are actually owned by a related party such as a spouse or a corporation you also own. Form 3520 is pertinent if you are the grantor or "substantial owner" of a foreign trust. While the word "trust" brings up the idea of wealthy families, the U.S. tax rules see products such as the Canadian RESP (similar to a U.S. 529 plan) or foreign retirement plans (similar to a 401(k)) as foreign trusts. Form 8621 is for people who own stock in a Passive Foreign Investment Company (PFIC). In many cases, foreign mutual funds would also be classified as PFIC.

My advice to everyone who does not already file is simple: you have a lot more to lose by not filing than by getting caught up with your taxes. You may not have to face the consequences of it today or tomorrow, but the longer you go without paying your legal dues, the more likely it is that it will eventually come back to bite you (and the worse the bite will be when it happens). Most people owe a lot less than they think they do, and getting compliant can be a much easier process than they assume.

In chapter 2, I'll show you exactly how to go from non-compliance to being totally compliant in the easiest (and cheapest) possible ways. While many people today rely on the IRS' standard interview process to file yearly, I hope to show you that it pays to go over everything with a fine-tooth comb and take advantage of every policy at your disposal when you file. Tax preparation software like TurboTax can certainly be useful for organizing your information, but one should always review the actual forms before filing.

INTRODUCTION TO FORM 1040

Before we get started, I want to introduce to the most important tax form of all. It's so important, in fact, that my company 1040 Abroad is named after it.

Form 1040 is your personal tax return. Your income, deductions and tax owing or tax refund will be shown here. Depending on the source of your income and whether you incurred expenses, you will need to attach the appropriate schedules (which I explain in the coming chapters).

The form begins by asking for all your personal details and filing status. Entering the wrong SSN number or omitting it entirely disqualifies your personal exemption, so pay close attention to detail here.

Exemptions	6a	☐ **Yourself.** If someone can claim you as a dependent, **do not** check box 6a					Boxes checked on 6a and 6b
	b	☐ **Spouse**					No. of children on 6c who:
	c	**Dependents:**	(2) Dependent's social security number	(3) Dependent's relationship to you	(4) ✓ if child under age 17 qualifying for child tax credit (see instructions)		• lived with you
		(1) First name Last name				☐	• did not live with you due to divorce or separation (see instructions)
If more than four dependents, see Instructions and check here ▶ ☐						☐	Dependents on 6c not entered above
	d	Total number of exemptions claimed					Add numbers on lines above ▶ ☐

Income	7	Wages, salaries, tips, etc. Attach Form(s) W-2		7	
	8a	Taxable interest. Attach Schedule B if required		8a	
Attach Form(s) W-2 here. Also attach Forms W-2G and 1099-R if tax was withheld.	b	Tax-exempt interest. **Do not** include on line 8a	8b		
	9a	Ordinary dividends. Attach Schedule B if required		9a	
	b	Qualified dividends	9b		
	10	Taxable refunds, credits, or offsets of state and local income taxes		10	
	11	Alimony received		11	
	12	Business income or (loss). Attach Schedule C or C-EZ		12	
	13	Capital gain or (loss). Attach Schedule D if required. If not required, check here ▶ ☐		13	
If you did not get a W-2, see instructions.	14	Other gains or (losses). Attach Form 4797		14	
	15a	IRA distributions 15a	b Taxable amount	15b	
	16a	Pensions and annuities 16a	b Taxable amount	16b	
	17	Rental real estate, royalties, partnerships, S corporations, trusts, etc. Attach Schedule E		17	
	18	Farm income or (loss). Attach Schedule F		18	
	19	Unemployment compensation		19	
	20a	Social security benefits 20a	b Taxable amount	20b	
	21	Other income. List type and amount		21	
	22	Combine the amounts in the far right column for lines 7 through 21. This is your **total income** ▶		22	

Here, you must report all your income. The schedules are used to provide greater detail about the numbers you input on Form 1040's lines. Remember, all monetary figures must be converted into U.S. dollars. See more in the Schedule D description that follows. On line 22, report your total income from all sources.

Adjusted Gross Income	23	Educator expenses	23	
	24	Certain business expenses of reservists, performing artists, and fee-basis government officials. Attach Form 2106 or 2106-EZ	24	
	25	Health savings account deduction. Attach Form 8889	25	
	26	Moving expenses. Attach Form 3903	26	
	27	Deductible part of self-employment tax. Attach Schedule SE	27	
	28	Self-employed SEP, SIMPLE, and qualified plans	28	
	29	Self-employed health insurance deduction	29	
	30	Penalty on early withdrawal of savings	30	
	31a	Alimony paid b Recipient's SSN ▶	31a	
	32	IRA deduction	32	
	33	Student loan interest deduction	33	
	34	Tuition and fees. Attach Form 8917	34	
	35	Domestic production activities deduction. Attach Form 8903	35	
	36	Add lines 23 through 35	36	
	37	Subtract line 36 from line 22. This is your **adjusted gross income** ▶		

The Adjusted Gross Income section of the form allows you to deduct eligible expenses you incurred during the year. Subtracting these deductions from your total income gives you the adjusted gross income that you'll be taxed on. This is the end of the first page of the Form 1040.

	38	Amount from line 37 (adjusted gross income)		
Tax and Credits	39a	Check if: ☐ **You** were born before January 2, 1952, ☐ Blind. ☐ **Spouse** was born before January 2, 1952, ☐ Blind. Total boxes checked ▶ 39a		
	b	If your spouse itemizes on a separate return or you were a dual-status alien, check here▶		39b☐
Standard Deduction for—	40	**Itemized deductions** (from Schedule A) or your **standard deduction** (see left margin)		
	41	Subtract line 40 from line 38		
• People who check any box on line 39a or 39b or who can be claimed as a dependent, see instructions.	42	**Exemptions.** If line 38 is $155,650 or less, multiply $4,050 by the number on line 6d. Otherwise, see instructions		
	43	**Taxable income.** Subtract line 42 from line 41. If line 42 is more than line 41, enter -0-		
	44	**Tax** (see instructions). Check if any from: a ☐ Form(s) 8814 b ☐ Form 4972 c ☐		
• All others:	45	**Alternative minimum tax** (see instructions). Attach Form 6251		
Single or Married filing separately, $6,300	46	Excess advance premium tax credit repayment. Attach Form 8962		
	47	Add lines 44, 45, and 46		▶
	48	Foreign tax credit. Attach Form 1116 if required	48	
Married filing jointly or Qualifying widow(er), $12,600	49	Credit for child and dependent care expenses. Attach Form 2441	49	
	50	Education credits from Form 8863, line 19	50	
	51	Retirement savings contributions credit. Attach Form 8880	51	
Head of household, $9,300	52	Child tax credit. Attach Schedule 8812, if required	52	
	53	Residential energy credits. Attach Form 5695	53	
	54	Other credits from Form: a ☐ 3800 b ☐ 8801 c ☐	54	
	55	Add lines 48 through 54. These are your **total credits**		
	56	Subtract line 55 from line 47. If line 55 is more than line 47, enter -0-		▶

The Tax and Credits section starts with your adjusted gross income. It is quite significant, as many limitations are based on this number. Here, we will adjust it even more. There are personal exemptions, as well as standard deductions and itemized deductions to further decrease your taxable income. If the amount of your incurred deductible expenses during the year is higher than the standard deduction, use this number to decrease your taxable income even further. If you use the itemized deduction, see the Schedule A instructions. This is also the part where you can claim the Foreign Tax Credit to offset your U.S. tax owing if you have paid taxes to a foreign country.

Other Taxes	57	Self-employment tax. Attach Schedule SE		57
	58	Unreported social security and Medicare tax from Form: a ☐ 4137 b ☐ 8919		58
	59	Additional tax on IRAs, other qualified retirement plans, etc. Attach Form 5329 if required		59
	60a	Household employment taxes from Schedule H		60a
	b	First-time homebuyer credit repayment. Attach Form 5405 if required		60b
	61	Health care: individual responsibility (see instructions) Full-year coverage ☐		61
	62	Taxes from: a ☐ Form 8959 b ☐ Form 8960 c ☐ Instructions; enter code(s) ___		62
	63	Add lines 56 through 62. This is your **total tax** ▶		63
Payments	64	Federal income tax withheld from Forms W-2 and 1099	64	
	65	2016 estimated tax payments and amount applied from 2015 return	65	
If you have a qualifying child, attach Schedule EIC.	66a	Earned income credit (EIC)	66a	
	b	Nontaxable combat pay election 66b		
	67	Additional child tax credit. Attach Schedule 8812	67	
	68	American opportunity credit from Form 8863, line 8	68	
	69	Net premium tax credit. Attach Form 8962	69	
	70	Amount paid with request for extension to file	70	
	71	Excess social security and tier 1 RRTA tax withheld	71	
	72	Credit for federal tax on fuels. Attach Form 4136	72	
	73	Credits from Form: a ☐ 2439 b ☐ Reserved c ☐ 8885 d ☐	73	
	74	Add lines 64, 65, 66a, and 67 through 73. These are your **total payments** ▶		74

Here are reported additional taxes that you cannot offset with the Foreign Tax Credit, such as self-employment tax or Net Investment Income Tax (NIIT). We will cover these in greater detail in the later chapters of this book. Pay particular attention to Line 61: health care. If you live abroad and don't pay Social Security, you will have to file Form 8965, Health Coverage Exemption, and check that you lived abroad during the year. There is a penalty for not having the health coverage exemption.

The next part of Form 1040 is for payments. A lot of people are not aware of the Additional Child Tax Credit, which you claim in this section on line 67. More information on this can be found in Chapter 5: Credits.

Refund	75	If line 74 is more than line 63, subtract line 63 from line 74. This is the amount you **overpaid**	75
	76a	Amount of line 75 you want **refunded to you**. If Form 8888 is attached, check here ▶ ☐	76a
Direct deposit? See Instructions.	b Routing number ▶	▶ c Type: ☐ Checking ☐ Savings	
	d Account number ▶		
	77	Amount of line 75 you want **applied to your 2017 estimated tax** ▶ 77	
Amount You Owe	78	Amount you owe. Subtract line 74 from line 63. For details on how to pay, see instructions ▶	78
	79	Estimated tax penalty (see instructions) 79	
Third Party Designee	Do you want to allow another person to discuss this return with the IRS (see instructions)? ☐ **Yes.** Complete below. ☐ No		
	Designee's name ▶	Phone no. ▶	Personal identification number (PIN) ▶
Sign Here Joint return? See instructions. Keep a copy for your records.	Under penalties of perjury, I declare that I have examined this return and accompanying schedules and statements, and to the best of my knowledge and belief, they are true, correct, and accurately list all amounts and sources of income I received during the tax year. Declaration of preparer (other than taxpayer) is based on all information of which preparer has any knowledge.		
	Your signature	Date	Your occupation	Daytime phone number
	Spouse's signature. If a joint return, **both** must sign.	Date	Spouse's occupation	If the IRS sent you an Identity Protection PIN, enter it here (see inst.)
Paid Preparer Use Only	Print/Type preparer's name	Preparer's signature	Date	Check ☐ if self-employed PTIN
	Firm's name ▶			Firm's EIN ▶
	Firm's address ▶			Phone no.

Lastly, if you paid too much tax, or you have no tax owing but you are eligible for claiming the Additional Child Tax Credit and you receive a refund, input the number on Line 76a of the Refund section. Calculate the tax owing, sign and send to the IRS.

HOW THIS BOOK IS STRUCTURED

In preparing this book, I have chosen to structure the chapters around the design of Form 1040, since it is effectively a summary of the entire tax return.

Chapter 1 is a simple introduction to the expatriate or perpetual traveler lifestyle, including the most important things I've learned and observed for making the most out of this innovative way to live.

Chapter 2 serves as an overview of the basics you will need to understand to move from non-compliance to full compliance, no matter how long it has been since you last filed (if ever). It will introduce you to the breadth of different types of circumstances you may be able to take advantage of with your filing.

Chapter 3 focuses on lines 7 through 21 of Form 1040, which pertain to income items. The Foreign Earned Income Exclusion is entered as a negative number on line 21, and as such it will also be covered here.

Moving on to Chapter 4, we will go over tax deductions. These are handled on lines 22 through 42 of Form 1040. The main topic will be the itemized deductions found on Schedule A.

In Chapter 5, I explain tax credits (lines 48 through 55). The main credit to be concerned with is the Foreign

Tax Credit, but the Additional Child Tax Credit could also be applicable to expats.

Chapter 6 is lines 57 through 63, relating to other types of taxes. I will discuss the Self-Employment Tax and PFIC tax here. The Affordable Care Act penalty for failing to have health insurance is also be reported in this section (but it is rarely applicable to expats).

Finally, in closing out Chapter 7, I will explain how and why you should consider renouncing your U.S. citizenship, thus ending your tax obligation to the IRS for good. I will also give you some guidance on what alternative citizenships to consider, whether or not you ever actually renounce.

Let's begin.

CHAPTER ONE

MOVING, LIVING &
WORKING ABROAD

If you are still in the planning stages of leaving the United States to begin your new life abroad, there are probably endless questions to intimidate and confuse you. Left unaddressed, they could greatly delay or even permanently halt your dreams of worldwide exploration. A lifestyle overseas will change a lot more than just the way you file your taxes, so it's important to understand the challenges and opportunities that may await you. These are things I've had to learn the hard way through my own experience as a nomad and expatriate – and which I've seen countless times in the lives of my clients, colleagues, and friends. They are the first obstacles you must learn to work with, well before you ever begin filling out your tax return.

THE DYNAMICS OF RELOCATING

Becoming an American expat or perpetual traveler can be disorienting and enlightening. You'll experience a wide range of lifestyles if you keep yourself open. Don't expect the privilege of being able to go about most of your day in an isolated bubble. Your presence will bring about lots of interaction and attention in some places. In the third world, the more you live like a local and skip the luxury items you might find at home, the further your dollar will go.

On the other hand, moving from the developing world to somewhere relatively wealthy can be very relaxing and liberating. But you may also feel like there is stronger pressure to conform to their more established cultural identity. Everyone's cup of tea is different, so if you've never traveled you may not know where your ideal destination lies.

On some level, we are all conscious of the cultural realms of the countries we choose to visit: formal, historical Europe... lively, humble Latin America... or crowded, collectivist Asia. You may feel a call to one of these places to prove or disprove what you feel. Nothing will offer you the complete picture until you live the experience for yourself. You may also be ready to drink in as many of these cultural biomes as you can. If covering as much of the globe as possible is a high priority on your bucket list, the destination of "nowhere in particular" is always available to you. In the age of Google, there are no careless whims or dark frontiers. A certain class of perpetual traveler is made possible by the remote working capabilities of the internet. With a little tech savvy and wise money management, you could become a digital nomad whose address is anywhere in the world with good Wifi.

The most widely shared quality among cultural differences is that they can be managed. Be real about your concerns. Laugh about your over corrections, and take credit for those strokes of quick thinking and luck that helped your adventures turn out more memorable (wherever you go in the world).

FAMILY DYNAMICS ABROAD

If you are already a seasoned traveler, you must keep in mind that just because you're adventurous and adaptable, it doesn't necessarily mean that your children or spouse are. Nor will they automatically pick these traits up from you. They likely value their existing stability and relationships. Communication and mutual respect are essential. As you start having the desire to relocate, you should communicate it so that you are on the same page with everyone in your family.

Even if you don't have kids and never want to, you may find that life on the road or under vastly different circumstances can be a great strain on your relationship with your spouse or partner. You won't have the freedom just to pack up and go wherever you want at a moment's notice unless your partner is in complete agreement.

Marrying a foreigner can bring opportunities regarding being able to immigrate to their country, and you would be a global couple from the start. Depending on your background though, you will also have to navigate sometimes significant cultural differences.

If children are in the works, their citizenship will depend on both the citizenship of their parents and their place of birth. In the United States and much of the Americas and British heritage countries, birthright citizenship (jus soli, "right of soil") is in effect.

By contrast, other countries such as France, Ireland or Italy rely more heavily on ancestry (jus sanguinis, "right of blood") to establish citizenship. Although, most countries will have some combination of these two.

To the extent that your children are U.S. citizens, you will receive an Additional Child Tax Credit at a rate of $1,000 per child per year (so long as you have at least $3,000 of earned income and do not take advantage of certain other options like the Foreign Earned Income Exclusion.

If your children are born outside the United States, they will automatically be considered U.S. citizens if they are either:

1. *born of two current U.S. citizens, or*
2. *born of one current U.S. citizen who has spent at least five years in the U.S. before the child's birth.*

Additionally, the U.S. Constitution makes every child born in the United States a U.S. citizen.

WORKING ABROAD

Your biggest concern about relocating might not have anything to do with overcoming cultural obstacles. You might be more focused on how you are supposed to make a living in a new country with its own laws, language, marketplace demands, and requirements. Many people in the modern age continue to work for a U.S. company while going wherever their heart desires. After all, why not? Most everything done in an office environment can be done online, from conferencing face-to-face to sending and signing documents. If you ever want to do this in a company that doesn't already practice this arrangement, consider actively demonstrating to your employer that working remotely won't be any functionally different to the operation of the company (or that your productivity could actually increase from home).

Personally, I have found that convincing an employer in most conventional workplaces to let you work on your own schedule from halfway around the world is too much of a cultural shock for them to handle. It is generally more favorable to create a living for yourself on your own terms. This also has an amplifying effect on the personal freedom most people are pursuing by going abroad in the first place. Alternatively, if you take your skills abroad to a foreign marketplace, you may suddenly find yourself in high demand in the job market.

Working for a larger foreign company is the easiest tax situation for Americans living abroad, and the most likely to cause you to avoid being liable to pay both income tax and Social Security. Being fully liable to both in a country with a higher tax rate and with a Social Security Totalization Agreement is another way to go about it. You may be surprised to find that some of the common-place skills and experience you have developed in your ordinary career at home are highly valued in certain other places. You could find yourself in a much higher-salaried position with the same qualifications simply by going where you are in greater demand.

If your goal is to start a new company and register it abroad, you can save on Social Security. You could simply create a foreign corporation with other Americans or by yourself. However, having more than 50% of the corporation owned by U.S. shareholders will make it a Controlled Foreign Corporation (which, as we will cover in the following chapters, is best avoided). As your business becomes more location independent, you will likely also have a greater pool of talent available for hire. Your money could go further – but you might have to spend more of it to overcome the shortcomings of the local infrastructure. The new variables to deal with are nearly endless but can be mastered with time. Just be aware that the way you are used to getting things done in the United States may not be appropriate in other places.

MAINTAINING TIES BACK HOME

The internet is crucial to nearly every location independent business. But copyright holders, local utilities, and governments all influence how the internet performs. In some places, like China or Iran, the internet is heavily censored to the great lament of foreigners. Virtual Private Networks, or VPNs, allow browsers to bypass geographical internet restrictions by masking your access in another location. Be warned that VPNs can range from secure and legitimate to sketchy and spammy. Unfortunately, the countries most notorious for Internet censorship are the ones that have the tightest restrictions on VPNs. Besides the regular VPN offers, roaming with your cell phone and tethering it to create a Wifi network is also a solution to borrow a remote I.P. address. Google's project Fi is interesting in that respect. A Hong Kong phone company also offers roaming in China, while maintaining a Hong Kong I.P. address.

If you're a perpetual traveler, you may want to consider a mailing address based in the U.S., for simplicity's sake. Paid services exist specifically for expats which mind your U.S. P.O. Box. They show you your mail, and let you decide whether they should forward it to you, scan it, or toss it. If you're addicted to Amazon.com and can't fathom living without easy access to online retail, a mail forwarding service like this can be invaluable. While scanning letters and receiving a pdf is easy enough, forwarding packages (or other physical products such as credit cards) can be trickier when moving too often means lacking a stable mailing address to actually receive it.

Having a U.S. based mailing address could also be part of your state taxation strategy. Not only will you be liable for income tax to the federal government, but the state where you were last a resident might continue to see you as such and expect you to pay state income tax. This would continue unless and until you sever your ties with that state. Although, many do offer some relief, either providing safe harbor to be treated as a non-resident, allowing some Foreign Tax Credit, or allowing the Foreign Earned Income Exclusion. Some do not offer any relief at all (yes, Pennsylvania, I am looking at you). The states of Alaska, Florida, Nevada, New Hampshire, South Dakota, Tennessee, Texas, Washington, and Wyoming do not have an income tax (although New Hampshire does have a tax on dividends and interest).

Common steps to move your residence to another state include registering to vote in the new state, getting a driver's license in that state, and maintaining a mailing address there.

I have been using www.travellingmailbox.com in many locations, but to establish an address in a no-income-tax state, you could also use any of the following services. You will need a notarized copy of your ID to open such a mailbox (PS Form 1583).

- *www.myrvmail.com* (Florida)
- *www.escapees.com* (Texas, Florida and South Dakota)
- *www.mydakotaaddress.com* (South Dakota)
- *www.sbimailservice.com* (Florida)
- *www.earthclassmail.com* (Texas, Florida, and Washington)
- *www.scanmailboxes.com* (Texas)

Additionally, if you need a non-US address, you can set up an address in Canada through www.canadianaddress.ca. Heavy usage can become prohibitively expensive ($3/letter), but it is a good backup address, with a personalized service. UK Post Box (www.ukpost-box.com) offers a similar service in the United Kingdom. Keeping a U.S. bank account while abroad will give you access to more ATMs and credit services. Banking is easily managed online nowadays, though you may find your debit card getting temporarily blocked every time you enter a new country without notifying your bank first. Many now offer services where customers can deposit checks by taking pictures of them. Most U.S. banks will serve customers with foreign mailing addresses. For day-to-day banking, though, and for purchases from stores that won't accept a foreign check, you'll want to establish an account with a reputable bank in your host country.

Another lifestyle factor to consider: your favorite American brands are all now suddenly imports. If you're a creature of comforts, expect to pay a little more in some cases. My preference for some products is what caused me to continue to use Amazon.com and U.S. eBay instead of their foreign site variations, but it also led me to have to forward packages too many times which had arrived at a destination after I had already left. You will also need the appropriate power adapters for the regions you visit, and to explore your cell phone's SIM card situation in every new country you go. I usually buy a new SIM card in every country I arrive in, before even leaving the airport, so that I can get online and make calls right away.

MITIGATING TRAVEL EXPENSES

I have not found travel expenses to be that significant. Although there are some new things you must pay for, this is countered by the fact that, unlike a vacation, you do not have to maintain two houses. You can save on tax and enjoy a cheaper cost of living if you adapt your way of life to a less expensive country. A plane ticket can also be amortized over time. You can buy a one-way ticket to stay in a location for a few months, not necessarily hopping from place to place every week.

Frequent flyer programs can also be a way to enjoy special perks. A U.S. credit history and mailing address can be handy.

Here are a few resources to help you to make the most of these programs:

- *www.awardwallet.com*: I use it to keep track of my various frequent flyer accounts.
- *www.flightfox.com*: Before buying a plane ticket, I check with them to see if they can find it cheaper. If they cannot beat the quoted price by more than their fee, they will refund you.
- *www.buyairlinemiles.com*: for buying miles.
- www.flyertalk.com: where travel deals show up first (warning: lots of content).
- *www.travelhacking.org*: a membership website created by Chris Guillebeau which curates all the best info from Flyertalk.
- *www.hotwire.com*: the best website for finding 3-star and above hotels for less. The catch is that you know the name of the hotel only after

the non-refundable booking has been made. Feeling adventurous?

- *www.priceline.com*: whereas Hotwire gives you a price, Priceline's "Name Your Own Price" feature lets you choose a price, which the hotel then accepts or declines.
- *www.prioritypass.com* and *www.loungeclub.com*: provide access to airport lounges. If you have good U.S. credit history, you should be able to find a credit card which provides this for free.
- *www.nomadlist.com*: various information (cost of living, internet speed, climate, and more) about the world's most popular long-term travel destinations to help digital nomads decide "where next?"

For those who can afford it, a hotel can be a comfortable way to celebrate the start of your stay. Hostels are much more affordable places, most with free maps, bread, and Wifi. But these communal lodgings can be cramped, chaotic, and of questionable security. When you've graduated past the dorm-like quality of the hostel and are looking for something more permanent, you can seek out an apartment or house rental recommendation from your local community of fellow expatriates online. They can hopefully recommend foreigner friendly accommodations within your price range.

The less you burden yourself with the possessions, the easier your travels will be. Be more discerning when packing your suitcase by selecting durable, easy-care, versatile clothing and other items. Pack light because almost everything you need can also be purchased locally when required.

For staying productive on the ground, airport lounges are conducive to quiet work during long layovers. Any modern city will offer many cafes and restaurant options with free Wifi. For those who can swing it, coworking spaces are rapidly becoming more popular. They offer high-quality office space, community events, and networking opportunities at daily or monthly membership rates.

EMIGRATING FROM THE U.S.

When you've become firm in your decision to leave the United States, it's time to start getting into the details you're going to need to know about legally entering another country. As a citizen of the United States, you are very privileged to own the 4th most powerful passport in the world[3]. It will get you into 174 nations as a tourist without requiring a visa ahead of time. Still, I will often go the extra step of getting a better visa and having fewer restrictions on my travel. For Thailand, a 6-month visa is available in your country of residence. China and India offer 10-year visas to U.S. citizens. An extra $50 will get you a 90-day visa in Nepal. If you plan to stay a long time or work in another country, you'll likely need to apply for an entrepreneur, employment, retirement visa, or another form of permanent residency. Should eventual

---

[3] Source: Henley & Partners Visa Restrictions Index 2016

citizenship be one of your goals, permanent residency is also generally what opens the door to naturalization.

Expatriate organizations often compile lists of accessible housing in urban neighborhoods that are friendly to foreigners. It can be a great comfort to find these enclaves, from which you can branch out into buying a home or stay and enjoy the changing faces. As for your house back in the U.S., a good property management company, or even Airbnb, can give you a steady side income.

Travelers with children must consider their education. International schools believe that their standards are superior to the educational standards of any particular country. Alternatively, some traveling parents of the very young are foregoing schooling altogether, in line with studies that propose a later school starting age. Lately, there has even emerged a growing movement of "world schoolers" – a form of homeschooling where the classroom is all over the world. This is the ideal situation for parents who want to keep maximum influence in their own offspring's education, and the world offers some amazing and unique educational opportunities for people at every age.

If you are still in school yourself, you can try to acquire a student visa in your destination country by enrolling in school. Transferrable credits mean you can pick up and continue your educational journey where you see fit – provided you're a fan of paperwork.

If possible, it is always wise to make an in-person visit to the place you're planning to relocate to before any long-term stays. It's the best way to get a handle on the safety of the area, as well as to avoid any disappointments with your living arrangements. You can use your vacation time away from your normal job to scope out parts of the world you've considered moving to. Then, when you've had ample time to make all the necessary arrangements, make the jump for good.

FOREIGN BANK ACCOUNTS & INCORPORATION

The list of potentially desirable options for banking and incorporation is long, but there are a few jurisdictions that stand out on my radar and I think should be addressed here.

Hong Kong is popularly cited as an ideal place to incorporate and bank. Singapore also holds high regard as being great for banking. However, Singapore is now almost entirely off limits to U.S. citizens because Singaporean banks don't want the hassle of FATCA reporting. If you are very wealthy (able to work with an opening deposit of $250,000 or more) or a legal resident of Singapore, you may be able to find banks who will make an exception for you.

Hong Kong is likewise now much harder to bank in than it used to be, but it is still possible for those with local operations. However, operating in Hong Kong would also subject you to Hong Kong income tax (15%). Hong Kong doesn't impose tax on those with no Hong Kong income, but it is getting much harder to qualify for this exception.

When it comes to ease of opening, Belize stands out. It is an easy place to incorporate and bank with no income tax. However, it lacks the prestige of other popular jurisdictions. If you incorporate there, prepare to bank there as well.

Like Belize, Georgia (the country, not the state) is a jurisdiction which makes it easy for foreigners to do business. One can open a bank account with just a passport, and they are quite happy to work with Americans despite the FATCA regulations.

Estonia is now offering an e-residency program, which is simply the issuance of an identity card which allows one to open and operate an Estonian corporation and bank account remotely. Estonia has a tax rate of 20%, but it only applies to earnings actually distributed (not to retained earnings staying within the corporation).

Finally, while it is tempting to shy away from first-world countries, British Columbia (in Canada) offers partnerships and corporations to non-residents. By paying out all the earnings in the form of wages to officers (i.e. you), you wouldn't have any tax to pay (if services were performed outside of Canada). However, the corporation would still have to file a tax return, and wages would be subject to reasonable compensation rules (neither of which would be issues in Belize).

CHAPTER TWO

GETTING AND STAYING TAX COMPLIANT

So... You've decided to file your U.S. taxes. Congratulations, and welcome to the club of tax compliant Americans abroad. Read on to find out exactly how to make that happen while preserving as much of your wealth and sanity as possible.

April 15 (or April 18 in 2017, taking into account the weekend and Emancipation Day[4]) is widely known as the due date for taxes. But the truth is that date only applies if you are living within the U.S. when it happens. If you're living in a foreign country on April 15, you have until June 15, 2017, to file. You do not need to file for this extension; it is automatically afforded to anybody living overseas. If you need even more time, you can apply for an extension that will give you until October 16, 2017, to file. No response from the IRS is needed. So long as you've sent off Form 4868 by the June or April due date, your late tax return is covered.

---

[4] A bank holiday in Washington DC falling on April 17 in 2017.

Please note, however, that the extensions are an extension to file, not an extension to pay. Interest on taxes owed starts accruing on April 15. If you suspect that you will owe tax, you can attach a payment to Form 4868.

If you have lived outside of the country most of the year, you can have up to $101,300 of your income excluded from federal taxes under the Foreign Earned Income Exclusion (FEIE) (Form 2555). You can also claim a credit for any taxes you have paid to foreign governments through the Foreign Tax Credit (FTC) (Form 1116). This is very useful if you are a resident or worker in another country. Generally speaking, if your foreign tax rate is greater than your U.S. tax rate, the FTC would be a more advantageous tactic to use. Otherwise, the FEIE is better.

In addition to these credits, it is important to establish your U.S. residence in a state which does not impose state income tax. Many states have tax laws that mirror the federal exclusions, allowing either the FEIE or FTC for state tax purposes. Others have so-called "safe harbor" laws - that is, you would be taxed as a non-resident even though you list your main residence in that state. They apply to people who have been out of the state for a specific number of days through the year, so it's important to keep track of where you were.

For instance, New York has developed a reputation for its "548 days" rule. Under this rule, if someone spends at least 450 days in a 548-day period in a foreign country and less than 90 days in New York, even though that person might otherwise be a resident they would be treated as a non-resident for tax purposes. Maine has a similar rule.

Ohio upholds the following safe harbor rule, which applies to anyone who meets all the following conditions:

(i) The individual spent less than 183 days in Ohio during the taxable year,

(ii) The individual has at least one abode outside this state during the entire taxable year (the law does not define "abode"),

(iii) The individual did not change domicile from or to Ohio during the taxable year (referred to as a part-year resident in the instructions to Form IT 1040),

(iv) By May 30 of the immediately succeeding calendar year the individual files the affidavit of non-Ohio domicile Form ITDA - NM (affidavit for nonmilitary), and:

(v) The affidavit does not contain any false statements.

If you're looking to change the state of your residence for tax purposes, keep in mind that some states do not collect income tax. To prove that you've established a new residence, however, you would need to re-register to vote, get a driver's license in the new state, and update your mailing address with your banks and other organizations. Getting a driver's license in the new state typically requires a visit to that state. There are a few mailbox services that not only provide you a mailing address in the new state but also guide you in the process. Virtual mailboxes which cater to people living in an RV have a greater focus on also helping you establish residency in your new state.

Expats with children take note - if you have a U.S. citizen child, you can get a refundable tax credit of $1,000 per year per child. This is called the "Additional Child Tax Credit." To qualify, you must have at least $3,000 of earned income and not use the Foreign Earned Income Exclusion.

PAPERWORK AND FORMS

Paperwork... the bane of taxpayers everywhere. Of course, when I say "paperwork" I don't just mean actual physical paper forms that must be completed, signed, and mailed in (though those are still quite often required in many tax situations). The paperwork also includes electronic files, pdfs, and anything you turn into the IRS containing your tax information. Although software exists to aid with electronic filing, many Americans abroad are not eligible for electronic filing.

The enormous amount of paperwork is already bad enough for Americans who live and earn their income within the borders of the U.S. In fact, the intimidating amount of paperwork involved, much of it totally indecipherable to the average American, is probably one of the most important unconscious barriers to people getting and staying tax compliant. After all, a single error on just one of many forms you'll likely need to fill out could lead to serious trouble with the IRS. It's a bizarre and stressful form of mental terror – and that's why

American society will always gainfully employ tax professionals.

For example, if you look at the bottom of the instructions for Form 8621 - Passive Foreign Investment Income (PFIC), you'll see that the estimated burden for all other taxpayers who file this form is 49 hours (just for this one form!). If you see PFIC, you might think that it is something that only wealthy people must deal with, but there is no de minimis rule in the case of sale of shares of a PFIC. Therefore, even a sale of a few hundred dollars would require that form. Failure to file this form means that the statute of limitations won't start (i.e. the IRS can audit you forever) and now also comes with the standard penalty for failure to file foreign related forms (i.e. $10,000). That's right: 49 hours just for one form.

As an American living abroad, you're going to have your own paperwork specific to your situation and your goals. It can be an overwhelming headache if you don't have some expert guidance to help you sort out the mess before you. In this chapter, I'll cover the basics of what you need to know here to make a little method out of the madness the IRS brings to your life each year with its endless paperwork.

When it comes to understanding the seemingly limitless slew of documents, I have found that the most important strategy is to be organized. I suggest looking at what information each form requires, and assembling the data before you begin the filing process. In my experience, the best strategy is to gather all the information in one place, preferably in a digital format. If you are a tax resident of a foreign country, you would gather information from your foreign employers and prepare a foreign tax return, which would then be your starting point for the preparation of your U.S. tax return. If you are self-employed, your starting point would be your bookkeeping system (such as Xero or Freshbooks). If you own a foreign corporation, it would be the financial statements for that corporation. When the correct numbers have been collected, going through the paperwork will be much less overwhelming.

It's important to note that all monetary figures must be given in U.S. dollars (unless otherwise specified, such as on Form 5471), no matter where you are in the world or in what currency you derive your income. For a lot of you, this means converting the income, currency, and value of assets to the U.S. dollar. Taxpayers can either use the exchange rate at the time you "receive, pay, or accrue the item" or the average exchange rate during the year. The average is generally used since it is much easier, and leads to a similar outcome. The exchange rate of any reliable source used consistently can be used. For capital gains, you would have to use the exchange rate on the day of the transaction. That may sound intimidating, but that's where I come in. I have spent many years of my life helping Americans abroad file taxes, and have yet to find a situation without a solution.

Remember, as an overseas resident, you get an automatic extension to June 15th, and can file for extensions up until October 15th if needed. The deadline to file an FBAR (report of non-US bank accounts) on form FinCEN 114 will match the due date of your tax return starting in 2017 (it used to be June 30). The IRS can claim half your bank account if you willfully fail to file an FBAR, so it's crucial to get these forms in.

Because having a bank account in the jurisdiction where you now live or work is so convenient, the majority of overseas residents will have to file an FBAR. Remember, having more than $10,000 (cumulatively in all your accounts at any time during the year) is what will cause you to have to file an FBAR. But certain other forms can apply to your situation as well. Generally, the IRS will pay more attention to accounts with large balances, situations with more entities involved, or instances in which the failure to file was willful. On that last point, in the age of FATCA, I strongly recommend against trying to hide your assets. It simply is not a sustainable strategy.

Whew. Still with me? It can be a lot to take in, but I promise to try to simplify things as much as possible for you in the following chapter as I cover the distinctions between the various forms you will need to know as you prepare to file. It's not as complicated as it seems at first glance.

The best way to explain the process is to include a real-life scenario of how I helped an expat who wanted to stay compliant while living overseas. Laura (not her real name) came to me last year as an American living abroad while teaching English in Milan. The move abroad was only temporary, so her home state of Ohio still considered her a local resident. Laura came to me for the same reason many people do: when it came to taxes, she didn't know where to start. She had earned income in both the United States and Italy and did not know which income she had to claim to each country. While the "tax season" can be daunting for many Americans abroad, I always strive to make the process more manageable for people in these kinds of situations.

Laura had to file for both state and federal taxes on the income she earned from writing magazine articles as a freelance writer. Although Laura was not physically in Ohio when she earned the money, she was still an Ohio resident. She still had to report her freelance income to Ohio. It is vital to check the status of your state of residence, as each varies widely. Some states allow taxpayers to use the Foreign Earned Income Exclusion for state purposes. Others allow a Foreign Tax Credit. Some others have some variation on a safe harbor rule, such as New York and the 548-day rule which states that if you spend more than 548 days in a foreign country, you will be taxed as a non-resident. Ohio has a weaker version of the safe harbor rule, which involves the filing of an affidavit and still requires you to establish ties in another state.

FTC & FEIE STATES

The following table should give you some guidelines as to which states allow Foreign Tax Credits or the Foreign Earned Income Exclusion. Please double check with the state's website to see exactly how it applies to your situation (for instance, Massachusetts only allows a Foreign Tax Credit for taxes paid to Canada).

State	Allows Foreign Tax Credits	Allows Foreign Earned Income Exclusion
Alabama	Yes	No
Alaska	No	Yes
Arizona	Yes	Yes
Arkansas	No	Yes
California	No	No
Colorado	No	Yes
Connecticut	No	Yes
Delaware	Yes	Yes
Florida	No	Yes
Georgia	No	Yes
Hawaii	Yes	No
Idaho	Yes	Yes
Illinois	No	Yes
Indiana	Yes	Yes
Iowa	Yes	Yes
Kansas	Yes	Yes
Kentucky	No	Yes
Louisiana	Yes	Yes
Maine	Yes	Yes
Maryland	No	Yes
Massachusetts	Yes	No

Michigan	Yes	Yes
Minnesota	Yes	Yes
Mississippi	No	Yes
Missouri	No	Yes
Montana	Yes	Yes
Nebraska	No	Yes
Nevada	No	Yes
New Hampshire	No	Yes
New Jersey	No	No
New Mexico	No	Yes
New York	Yes	Yes
North Carolina	Yes	Yes
North Dakota	No	Yes
Ohio	No	Yes
Oklahoma	No	Yes
Oregon	Yes	Yes
Pennsylvania	No	No
Rhode Island	No	Yes
South Carolina	No	Yes
South Dakota	No	Yes
Tennessee	No	Yes
Texas	No	Yes
Utah	No	Yes
Vermont	Yes	Yes

Virginia	Yes	Yes
Washington	No	Yes
West Virginia	No	Yes
Wisconsin	No	Yes
Wyoming	No	Yes

FORM 3520

Form 3520 is the Annual Return to Report Transactions with Foreign Trusts and Receipt of Certain Foreign Gifts. You must file this form if you are the grantor or "substantial owner" of a foreign trust. If you received over $100,000 from a foreign individual or over $15,601 from a foreign corporation, you would also have to file this form. A common example of a foreign trust is the Registered Education Savings Plan. The RESP was established by parents wanting to send their children to university in Canada. Any payouts a student receives must be claimed on Form 3520. Pension plans similar to a 401(k) ("defined contribution plan") might be treated the same way. Tax treaties might exempt one from this requirement, as would be the case with Canadian RRSPs.

FORM 5471

Form 5471 applies to you if either:
- You have bought or sold shares of a foreign corporation (during the tax year in question),

causing you to own at least 10% of the corporation, or

- if you own at least 10% of a Controlled Foreign
Corporation (CFC), then you must file Form
5471 for every year that continues to be true. A
CFC is a foreign corporation in which "U.S. shareholders" own at least 50% of the corporation. A
U.S. shareholder is defined as a U.S. person who
owns at least 10% of a foreign corporation.

PFICs & FORM 8621

Form 8621 deals with Passive Foreign Investment
Companies, or PFICs. These could include foreign mutual funds and other investment vehicles. Unlike the
other forms covered here, it has no minimum threshold.
The PFIC tax regimes and the excess distribution regime
are punitive tax rules. Investing outside the U.S. is too big
a subject to cover here, but it's one many people are
growing more and more concerned with every passing
tax year. If you need help figuring out the best way to
invest outside the U.S., my suggestion would be to read
the articles on www.1040abroad.com or contact me directly through there.

FBAR & FORM 8938

Americans need to file form FinCEN 114 (the FBAR
form) if they have more than $10,000 in foreign bank ac-
counts at any point in the year ($10,000 being the sum of
the aggregate balance of their bank accounts). They also

need to file Form 8938 if the value of their offshore assets is $200,000 or more on the final day of the tax year, or $300,000 anytime throughout the year (though this amount is higher for married couples who file jointly – lower filing thresholds apply to those who reside within the United States). Assets reported on Form 8938 include bank accounts and interests in foreign entities (such as trusts, partnerships, or corporations). The FBAR is far more common due to its much lower threshold. It is a form I help my clients fill out every year.

Last year, a man named Will reached out to me for help with his taxes. He was living in Canada with his wife, who was a non-resident alien not involved in the U.S. tax system. After incorrectly filing the previous years, he asked me for assistance. He had an email from an accountant erroneously claiming that the FBAR no longer existed and had been replaced by Form 8938. This bad advice from a professional ended up being vital to his ability to avoid paying a penalty since he now had "reasonable cause." He now needed to fill out an FBAR because he had bank accounts in Canada with an aggregate balance of more than $10,000. The form itself can be filled out online and is fairly simple to complete. The most pressing information with the FBAR involves knowing exactly what to include as an asset.

What you are required to claim on the FBAR:
- Foreign accounts where you have financial interest or authority of signature.
- Financial accounts in a foreign branch of a U.S. financial institution.
- Foreign mutual funds.

- Foreign-issued life insurance or annuity contract.

What you are not required to claim on the FBAR:
- Domestic mutual funds that invest in foreign stocks.
- Personal property held directly.
- Regulated financial accounts such as TFSA and RESP in Canada or Livret A in France.

Again, this process is made easier if you (forgive the pun) take into account all your investments and belongings.

OTHER IMPORTANT FORMS

Schedule A is the form you'll use to deduct your itemized expenses, such as mortgage interest, property taxes, medical expenses, and charitable contributions. Note that only charitable contributions to U.S. and Canadian charities are deductible. Using this form is beneficial when your itemized deduction amount is more than the standard deduction, which is $6,300 for a single person or $12,600 for a married couple filing jointly in 2015 and 2016.

Schedule B is used to report taxable interest and dividends. You must fill out Part III of the form if at any point during the tax year you've had a foreign financial account (e.g. a bank account, securities account, or brokerage account).

Schedule C is used to report the income (and deductible expenses) for your self-employment activity during the tax year.

Schedule D is where you report the capital gains and losses on your investments such as stock sales.

Schedule SE computes your self-employment tax, which comes into play when you cannot claim the benefits of a Social Security Totalization Agreement.

Form 8938 is the Statement of Specified Foreign Assets. Filing this form does not replace your obligation to file an FBAR. You need to check whether your foreign financial assets are subject to these reporting requirements and if they exceed certain financial thresholds. The threshold can vary. For an unmarried taxpayer residing outside the United States, the total value of assets is set at $200,000 or more on the last day of the tax year or more than $300,000 during the year. For married taxpayers residing outside the United States and filing jointly, the threshold is $400,000 on the last day of the year or $600,000 at any time during the year.

Form 8854 is known as the Initial and Annual Expatriation Statement. It is used by people who have renounced their U.S. citizenship or ended their long-term resident status to confirm that they are compliant with the U.S. tax system. The United States is the most expensive country in the world to renounce citizenship from. You might also be subject to an exit tax. The IRS requires five years of tax returns to avoid covered expatriate status, and you would attach Form 8854 to your final return. This will be covered more in Chapter 7: How and Why to Surrender U.S. Citizenship

Now, continue to Chapter 3, where we will discuss income.

CHAPTER THREE

INCOME

Income seems simple to understand at first glance, but from the point of view of the U.S. government, it can get fairly complicated. This applies doubly so to Americans earning their income from overseas. This chapter will focus on the main types of income encountered by U.S. citizens living outside the United States. Before seeing income types in detail (which each have their own forms), I first want to discuss a few things more generally.

Wages found on line 7 of Form 1040 would include all types of wages. They would be reported here regardless of whether Form W-2 was issued or not, whether these wages were U.S. sourced or foreign sourced, and whether the Foreign Earned Income Exclusion or the Foreign Tax Credit were used. I've seen too many instances of taxpayers preparing their own tax returns and making the same simple mistakes over and over. Most frequently, they report their wages on line 21 alongside the Foreign Earned Income Exclusion. Or worse, they simply reported the Foreign Earned Income Exclusion and didn't report the wages (resulting in a negative total income).

Rental income, as well as income from partnerships, would be reported on Schedule E and flow to line 17 of Form 1040.

Then, as IRC section 61 states, all income is taxable, unless otherwise specifically exempt. This means that any other income would end up on line 21 of Form 1040, I frequently see government grants and subsidies provided by foreign governments mistakenly end up here.

Of course, line 21 is also where you would report the Foreign Earned Income Exclusion, Subpart F Income, as well as income from PFICs (excess distribution) allocable to the current year. Don't worry. We'll go over this in greater detail later in the book.

SCHEDULE B

Use Schedule B to report your interest and dividend income during the tax year. Generally, you don't need to file the form unless your dividend and interest income exceed $1,500 and you have no foreign financial assets. However, if you live abroad and you have a bank account in a foreign country, you must complete Part III of Schedule B. Bear in mind that even if your earned interest and dividends are smaller than $1,500, you still must report this income on your personal tax return. But you might not have to complete Schedule B.

If you need to file Schedule B, enter the name of the payer and the amount paid to you on the appropriate lines. If you require more space, attach a statement to the return in the same format as Schedule B listing the details of the other payers. Enter the total on Schedule B.

Interest Income

In most cases, the interest you earn on your bank savings account, corporate bonds, or similar is subject to federal tax in the United States. There are some exceptions regarding this type of income, so the interest you earn on Series I or EE savings bonds (issued after 1989) can be excluded from your tax return.

SCHEDULE B (Form 1040A or 1040) Department of the Treasury Internal Revenue Service (99)	Interest and Ordinary Dividends ► Attach to Form 1040A or 1040. ► Information about Schedule B and its instructions is at www.irs.gov/scheduleb.	OMB No. 1545-0074 2015 Attachment Sequence No. 08
Name(s) shown on return		Your social security number

Part I Interest	1	List name of payer. If any interest is from a seller-financed mortgage and the buyer used the property as a personal residence, see instructions on back and list this interest first. Also, show that buyer's social security number and address ►		Amount
(See instructions on back and the instructions for Form 1040A, or Form 1040, line 8a.) Note: If you received a Form 1099-INT, Form 1099-OID, or substitute statement from a brokerage firm, list the firm's name as the payer and enter the total interest shown on that form.			1	
	2	Add the amounts on line 1	2	
	3	Excludable interest on series EE and I U.S. savings bonds issued after 1989. Attach Form 8815	3	
	4	Subtract line 3 from line 2. Enter the result here and on Form 1040A, or Form 1040, line 8a . . . . ►	4	
		Note: If line 4 is over $1,500, you must complete Part III.		Amount

If a U.S. financial institution paid the interest, your taxable interest can be found on Form 1099-INT given by the institution that you receive the interest from. Form 1099-INT contains all the information you need to determine whether you need to file the Schedule B or not and what amounts to report. Else, you would find it in the foreign equivalent (T3 or T5 in Canada) or directly from your financial institution.

Dividend Income

There are two types of dividends: ordinary dividends and qualified dividends. Ordinary dividends are taxed at ordinary rates whereas qualified dividends are taxed at

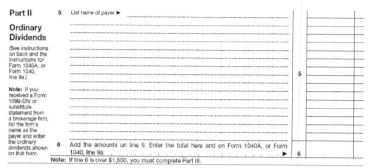

long-term capital gain rates (0/15/20%). If these are paid by a foreign payer, in many cases, they would still be qualified dividends by using a treaty making the payer a "Qualified Foreign Corporation." You would provide the name of the dividend payer on Schedule B and enter the dividends - if qualified, the amount would also be reported on Form 1040, line 9b.

If the payer is a U.S. company, you will receive Form 1099-DIV at the end of the tax year with all the necessary information required to complete Schedule B. If foreign, the foreign equivalent and the treaty to see if it qualifies as a qualified dividend.

Foreign Accounts and Trusts

This section must be filled if you have a foreign bank account or trust. Part III of Schedule B must also be completed if you have enough income from interest and dividends requiring you to file Schedule B.

			Yes	No
	You must complete this part if you (a) had over $1,500 of taxable interest or ordinary dividends; (b) had a foreign account; or (c) received a distribution from, or were a grantor of, or a transferor to, a foreign trust.			
Part III **Foreign** **Accounts** **and Trusts** (See instructions on back.)	**7a** At any time during 2015, did you have a financial interest in or signature authority over a financial account (such as a bank account, securities account, or brokerage account) located in a foreign country? See instructions			
	If "Yes," are you required to file FinCEN Form 114, Report of Foreign Bank and Financial Accounts (FBAR), to report that financial interest or signature authority? See FinCEN Form 114 and its instructions for filing requirements and exceptions to those requirements			
	b If you are required to file FinCEN Form 114, enter the name of the foreign country where the financial account is located ▶ _____			
	8 During 2015, did you receive a distribution from, or were you the grantor of, or transferor to, a foreign trust? If "Yes," you may have to file Form 3520. See instructions on back . . .			

For Paperwork Reduction Act Notice, see your tax return instructions. Cat. No. 17146N Schedule B (Form 1040A or 1040) 2015

If you hold foreign trusts, you might also have to file an additional Form 3520 and Form 3520A

SCHEDULE C

Schedule C is used to report income or loss from a business you operated during the tax year as a sole proprietor or U.S. single-member limited liability company (LLC) taxed as a disregarded entity. The taxpayer reports the business income on his personal tax return. If you run a business with your spouse, you might still be able to report half of it on Schedule C under the "joint venture exception," otherwise a partnership (or an LLC with multiple members) would be taxed as a partnership. In this case, the partnership would report its income on Form 1065 and issue forms K-1 to its partners, who would then report the income on their individual income tax returns.

Joint venture exception: If two spouses operate a business together, they can each directly report half of the income and expenses on Schedule C of their individual returns (treating it as a sole proprietorship instead of a partnership). Note that the joint venture exception is not available if the business is an LLC (it is only available to unincorporated businesses).

Small businesses with expenses amounting to $5,000 or less might file Schedule C-EZ instead. You'll find more information about Schedule C-EZ later in this chapter.

The first part of Schedule C is for general information about your business.

SCHEDULE C (Form 1040)	Profit or Loss From Business (Sole Proprietorship)	OMB No. 1545-0074
Department of the Treasury Internal Revenue Service (99)	▶ Information about Schedule C and its separate instructions is at www.irs.gov/schedulec. ▶ Attach to Form 1040, 1040NR, or 1041; partnerships generally must file Form 1065.	2015 Attachment Sequence No. 09

Name of proprietor	Social security number (SSN)

A	Principal business or profession, including product or service (see instructions)	B Enter code from instructions ▶
C	Business name. If no separate business name, leave blank.	D Employer ID number (EIN), (see instr.)
E	Business address (including suite or room no.) ▶ City, town or post office, state, and ZIP code	
F	Accounting method: (1) ☐ Cash (2) ☐ Accrual (3) ☐ Other (specify) ▶	
G	Did you "materially participate" in the operation of this business during 2015? If "No," see instructions for limit on losses	☐ Yes ☐ No
H	If you started or acquired this business during 2015, check here	▶ ☐
I	Did you make any payments in 2015 that would require you to file Form(s) 1099? (see instructions)	☐ Yes ☐ No
J	If "Yes," did you or will you file required Forms 1099?	☐ Yes ☐ No

You'll need to provide the principal business or profession, name and address of your business if it's different from your name, employer ID number (EIN), or your SSN, as well as state the accounting method you're using to report your business transactions.

The cash method is used when you report your transactions whenever cash is received or paid, while the accrual method is based on reporting the value of the business transaction as it occurs (regardless of whether the payment has been made or received).

Part I	Income		
1	Gross receipts or sales. See instructions for line 1 and check the box if this income was reported to you on Form W-2 and the "Statutory employee" box on that form was checked ▶ ☐	1	
2	Returns and allowances	2	
3	Subtract line 2 from line 1	3	
4	Cost of goods sold (from line 42)	4	
5	Gross profit. Subtract line 4 from line 3	5	
6	Other income, including federal and state gasoline or fuel tax credit or refund (see instructions)	6	
7	Gross income. Add lines 5 and 6 ▶	7	

Here you will report the gross business income during the tax year. Your sales returns of your damaged or unwanted products and allowances should be reported as a positive number on line 2.

Part II Expenses. Enter expenses for business use of your home only on line 30.

8	Advertising	8		18	Office expense (see instructions)	18
9	Car and truck expenses (see instructions)	9		19	Pension and profit-sharing plans	19
10	Commissions and fees	10		20	Rent or lease (see instructions):	
11	Contract labor (see instructions)	11		a	Vehicles, machinery, and equipment	20a
12	Depletion	12		b	Other business property	20b
13	Depreciation and section 179 expense deduction (not included in Part III) (see instructions)	13		21	Repairs and maintenance	21
				22	Supplies (not included in Part III)	22
				23	Taxes and licenses	23
				24	Travel, meals, and entertainment:	
14	Employee benefit programs (other than on line 19)	14		a	Travel	24a
15	Insurance (other than health)	15		b	Deductible meals and entertainment (see instructions)	24b
16	Interest:			25	Utilities	25
a	Mortgage (paid to banks, etc.)	16a		26	Wages (less employment credits)	26
b	Other	16b		27a	Other expenses (from line 48)	27a
17	Legal and professional services	17		b	Reserved for future use	27b
28	Total expenses before expenses for business use of home. Add lines 8 through 27a . . . ▶					28
29	Tentative profit or (loss). Subtract line 28 from line 7 .					29
30	Expenses for business use of your home. Do not report these expenses elsewhere. Attach Form 8829 unless using the simplified method (see instructions). Simplified method filers only: enter the total square footage of: (a) your home: and (b) the part of your home used for business: _____ Use the Simplified Method Worksheet in the instructions to figure the amount to enter on line 30 . . .					30
31	Net profit or (loss). Subtract line 30 from line 29. • If a profit, enter on both Form 1040, line 12 (or Form 1040NR, line 13) and on Schedule SE, line 2. (If you checked the box on line 1, see instructions). Estates and trusts, enter on Form 1041, line 3. • If a loss, you must go to line 32.					31

The second part of Schedule C is for expenses that your business incurred during the year. You will need to calculate the cost of goods sold and evaluate your ending inventory to calculate your gross profit. In this part, you can also deduct other business expenses such as advertising, wages, salaries, payroll expenses, the employer's taxes paid and vehicle expenses (providing you have additional information to support your deduction). Schedule C allows you to also deduct other expenses such as your cell phone, website expenses, part of your home if you're using it regularly and exclusively as a home office and other miscellaneous expenses.

28	Total expenses before expenses for business use of home. Add lines 8 through 27a . . . . ▶		28
29	Tentative profit or (loss). Subtract line 28 from line 7		29
30	Expenses for business use of your home. Do not report these expenses elsewhere. Attach Form 8829 unless using the simplified method (see instructions). Simplified method filers only: enter the total square footage of: (a) your home: and (b) the part of your home used for business: _____ Use the Simplified Method Worksheet in the instructions to figure the amount to enter on line 30		30
31	Net profit or (loss). Subtract line 30 from line 29. • If a profit, enter on both Form 1040, line 12 (or Form 1040NR, line 13) and on Schedule SE, line 2. (If you checked the box on line 1, see instructions). Estates and trusts, enter on Form 1041, line 3. • If a loss, you must go to line 32.		31
32	If you have a loss, check the box that describes your investment in this activity (see instructions). • If you checked 32a, enter the loss on both Form 1040, line 12, (or Form 1040NR, line 13) and on Schedule SE, line 2. (If you checked the box on line 1, see the line 31 instructions). Estates and trusts, enter on Form 1041, line 3. • If you checked 32b, you must attach Form 6198. Your loss may be limited.	32a ☐ All investment is at risk. 32b ☐ Some investment is not at risk.	

In the last part, you need to add up all your expenses on Line 28 and subtract this number from your gross income (Line 7) to get your Net Profit or Loss. You must report this number on your income tax return, Form 1040, Line 12.

If you have more than one business, you will have file a Schedule C for each of your businesses and then add up the income from them to report on Line 12 of Form 1040.

Refer to Chapter 6 for more information on the Self-Employment tax (Social Security's version for self-employed people). This tax may well be applicable to you if you filed Schedule C.

SCHEDULE D

Schedule D is used to report gain or loss on the sale or exchange of capital assets such as stocks, cars, houses, bonds, etc. Let's review some basic terminology to fully understand how we are calculating capital gains.

The basis is the amount you paid to acquire a particular asset (cost). Adjusted basis includes the money you spent on the asset during the holding period. You need to know the basis to figure out the capital gain or loss.

Proceeds are the price of the assets sold (the amount received from the sale).

When the holding period for assets is one year or less, they are short-term capital gains. The first part of the Schedule D focuses entirely on these. You must report the price of the assets acquired if it happened outside the U.S. in a foreign currency use the exchange rate from the date of acquisition. Report the date of the acquisition, the sales price (converted into U.S. dollars on the day the asset is sold), and calculate the gain or loss.

When the holding period for assets is more than one year, they are considered long-term capital gains. There's a lower tax rate for long-term capital gains.

Schedule D is used to report capital gains or losses. In many cases, you may have to use Form 8949 before completing Schedule D[5]. The gains you report are subject to the income tax. The tax rate differs whether the asset was held for a short or long time period. Losses on assets held for personal use are usually not deductible. However, in general, you can deduct capital losses up the amount of your capital gains plus $1,500 ($3,000 for married couples filing jointly) and capital losses above that limit can be carried over to future years.

Do you still remember what a Controlled Foreign Corporation is? It is any corporation in which more than 50% of the value or the voting power belongs to U.S. shareholders. A U.S. shareholder is a U.S. person who owns 10% or more of the voting power or value of the company.

Until 1962, U.S. investors could invest money in a foreign corporation and defer the income tax until the income was distributed as dividends, or even better, when the corporation was sold (and take advantage of the lower tax rate for long-term capital gains). Such practices were seen as particularly abusive when the foreign corporation wasn't a genuine business. Many corporations were just used as investment holding companies. U.S. taxpayers created the corporations in low- or no-tax jurisdictions and transferred investments to them, guaranteeing that the income would be taxed at a low rate or not at all until it was repatriated to its U.S. shareholders.

---

[5] Form 8949 reports the details of such transactions, which are then aggregated on Schedule D.

In other instances, a genuine business might exist, but the profit might be distorted by transfer pricing or other means. Imagine a U.S. company producing toys for pets. They create a subsidiary in a common low-tax haven, such as Panama. The subsidiary company won't be subject to income tax in Panama (under Panamanian territorial taxation). The U.S. parent company sells the toys at the cost of manufacturing, thus reporting no profit for the tax year. No profit means no tax owing to the U.S. government. The subsidiary in Panama exports the toys to Europe and receives tax-free income in return. The retained earnings stay within the subsidiary without being taxed (or are taxed at a lower rate).

As all U.S. persons are taxed on all their worldwide income, the U.S. government obviously does not like this tax loophole. The taxes on the Panamanian corporation's earnings went directly to the government of Panama. The U.S. cannot impose taxes on a foreign corporation without income being sourced from or otherwise engaging in U.S. based activities.

In response to this issue, Congress enacted Subpart F provisions to eliminate the deferral of tax on some categories of foreign income. These new rules required U.S. shareholders to report and be taxed on controlled foreign corporations, even if the CFC did not distribute any profits (I.R.C. § 951(a)). Every U.S. person holding at least 10% voting power of the value of the CFC must include the pro rata share of retained profits and earnings (known as Subpart F Income).

Subpart F Income increases the shareholder's basis. Any distributions decrease the basis.

SCHEDULE E

Schedule E is used to report rental income on a home or building, or receive royalties or income from a partnership, S corporation, trust or estate. You must report all income and expenses incurred during the tax year and attach it to your personal tax return.

Bear in mind that individuals, estates, and trusts might also cause you to pay the Net Investment Income Tax (NIIT), which is 3.8% of the lesser of the net investment income or the excess of modified adjusted income. Net investment includes rental and royalty income, as well as partnership or S corporation income. To determine your net investment tax, use Form 8960.

Schedule E is most commonly used to report rental properties income. You might be subject to self-employment tax if you manage rental properties as your main business activities. In this case, you will have to file Schedule C instead of Schedule E.

Let's look at how to complete Schedule E.

The first part is concerned with the details of the rental property, its address, the number of days it has been rented out, the type of property it is and the amount of income collected. You should also report here the income from any royalties you have received.

Expenses are reported on lines 5 through 21 for each property in the appropriate column. You can deduct taxes, interest, repair, insurance, management fees, depreciation, etc. In general, all ordinary and necessary expenses are deductible. However, you cannot deduct the value of your own labor or investments in the property (the later will be depreciated over a period of time).

PARTNERSHIPS & S CORPORATIONS

Partners of partnerships and shareholders of S corporations report their earned income on Schedule E, Part II. If you are a partner in a U.S. partnership, you should receive a Form K-1 that reports your share of the income, losses and deductions. If you have an S corporation, the S corporation must give you a K-1. Transfer these figures to your Schedule E and report it on your personal tax return as other income on Line 21.

Schedule E also allows you to deduct losses incurred in your particular business activity. However, the IRS limits the deductible loss to the amount that is "at-risk." The amount of losses incurred above the "at-risk" amount is not deductible.

Part III of Schedule E is used to report the income or loss from a fiduciary, so if you are a beneficiary of an estate or trust, you must file Schedule E regardless whether you received income or not. All the information you report in Part III can be found on Form K-1 provided by the fiduciary.

FORM 5471

This form is designed for U.S. persons who own shares of controlled foreign corporations, as well as for U.S. persons who acquire shares and then own more than 10% of the outstanding shares (and in some cases officers and directors of such corporations). It is an informational form that you must file even if there's no taxable income to report. It could also be used to report some income on the taxpayer's return (Subpart F Income, which we will discuss soon).

Once U.S. shareholders own more than 50% of a foreign corporation, the company is a Controlled Foreign Corporation (CFC). The Internal Revenue Code defines a U.S. shareholder as a U.S. person who holds 10% or more of the foreign corporation's voting power or value. Failing to file this form means the potential for hefty penalties, and the penalties can be assessed for each form filed late, incomplete, or inaccurate. What's more, if you fail to file Form 5471, you'll lose the statute of limitations and your tax returns will remain open for audit indefinitely, instead of just three or six years. The penalty starts at $10,000 for failure to file Form 5471 on time. If the IRS sends you a notice, a penalty of $10,000 is imposed for each 30-day period that you fail to file this form and an additional maximum penalty of $50,000. Bear in mind that even if you only have 10 percent of the value of the CFC, you're still legally obligated to file this form.

Form 5471 requires different schedules depending on your situation - the most comprehensive being in the case of someone owning more than 50% of a foreign corporation.

While preparing Form 5471, you might encounter the term "Subpart F Income", which must be reported on your personal tax return. The rules governing Subpart F Income are rather complex. I want you to know that it was designed to prevent tax avoidance on easily portable income associated with CFCs. In the past, U.S. investors could transfer assets to a foreign corporation. Without Subpart F rules, this income wouldn't be taxed until either dividends were paid to the taxpayer or the shares of the foreign corporation were sold (and then qualifying for long-term capital gain rates). Therefore, Congress passed Subpart F tax rules and implemented Form 5471 to reflect it and prevent tax evasion. Even though you might not be receiving any distribution from your foreign corporation, you are still subject to U.S. tax on your share of the Subpart F Income.

There is a lot of confusion related to the classification of the category of filers, treatment of a foreign company, and ownership in international law. Determining whether the taxpayer is required to file the form and which category he or she falls into is the first obstacle since not only the owners of a controlled foreign corporation are required to file the form. In some cases, an indirect owner (based on constructive ownership among family members or through the entities controlled by the taxpayer that have an interest in a CFC) might be obligated to file the form as well. For category 2, many believe that the regulations do not comply with the Internal Revenue Code. I'll spare you the details, but it is a complex topic indeed.

If you have an interest in a CFC, it would be highly pertinent for you to get in touch with a CPA specializing in international taxation for Americans.

UNDERSTANDING SUBPART F INCOME

Until 1962, one could create a foreign corporation and defer taxation on its income (especially passive income) until the corporation was sold. Furthermore, it would convert regular income into long-term capital gains (taxed at a lower tax rate). Congress passed provisions to prevent this deferral. The part of this code that does the excluding is called Subpart F. The basic premise is that income earned by the corporation is taxed to the shareholder even if it was not distributed.

Enacted in 1962, Subpart F tightly regulates income earned by Controlled Foreign Corporations. The two broad categories of income classified as Subpart F Income include income earned outside the company's country of incorporation ["Foreign base company income (FBCI)"] and passive income ["Foreign personal holding company income (FPHC)"]

Whether the income is from rents, royalties, interest, dividends, sales or services, you will end up owing under Subpart F. To the extent that these gains were not distributed, they would have to be listed as part of your individual return. There are a few exceptions to this rule. For instance, if you paid taxes to a foreign country equal to 90% of what you would pay in the U.S., it is not considered Subpart F Income (since the top tax rate is 39.8%, that means a foreign tax rate of 35.82% or greater). Also, regular operating income earned within the country of incorporation is not considered Subpart F Income, but importantly, the work you performed for the corporation ("Personal Services Income") is.

The Foreign Tax Credit applies to any taxes the CFC may have paid to its host country – the taxpayer can claim his/her share of FTC as if he/she had paid it himself/herself.

Another thing to watch out for is the fact that the sale of real estate is taxable under U.S. tax rules. In many countries, these sales may be tax-free. As such, you wouldn't be able to offset it with a Foreign Tax Credit. There are some notable exceptions available on the U.S. side, but it should ideally be broken down on a case-by-case basis. If you're not sure if there are any exceptions which apply specifically to you, contact me through my website and we'll go over your situation together, so that nothing will be missed.

Digital nomads can avoid having to pay into Social Security by being the employee of their own foreign corporation. The wage would equal what would otherwise be net income, and as such, there wouldn't be any income to be treated as Subpart F Income. It would otherwise be Subpart F Income – "Personal Services Income" to be specific.

WHAT QUALIFIES AS SUBPART F INCOME?

Subpart F Income is a set of new categories of income that taxpayers must include on their personal tax return. It is income generated by the corporation which would have to be included in the personal tax return of the U.S. shareholder. These are the categories are most subject to abuse through deferral of income to Controlled Foreign Corporations. Code section 951 requires that, under certain conditions, profits of a CFC must be treated as dividends and reported on U.S. shareholder's personal tax returns.

Categories that qualify as Subpart F Income include:

1. Insurance Income. Insurance income generated outside the country of incorporation.
2. Foreign Base Company Income
- Foreign Personal Holding Company Income (IRC 954(c)).

This is income derived mainly from investment income, such as dividends, capital gains, property transactions, foreign currency gains, commodity transactions, and personal service contracts[6]. Personal service contracts are applicable when the service is provided personally by a U.S. shareholder owning at least 25% of the corporation.

- Foreign Base Company Income (IRC 954 (d)).

---

[6] Personal Service Contracts (IRC 954(c)(1)(H)) amount received when the client personally contracts for services to be provided by a given person, or the service provider owns at least 25% of the CFC.

This rule oversees transactions outside the country of incorporation between related persons[7]. The income derived from these transactions is regarded as Subpart F Income.

- Foreign Base Company Sales Income (IRC 954 (d)).

This provision applies to related persons buying or selling property outside the country of incorporation.

- Foreign Base Company Service Income (IRC 954(e)). Only certain personal services such as technical, managerial, engineering, commercial, skilled, etc. are considered Subpart F Income. The service must be performed by or on behalf of a related person and performed outside the country of incorporation.

- Foreign Base Company Oil Related Income

This applies to the sale of oil that comes from outside the country of incorporation.

- Foreign Personal Holding Company Income

Foreign Personal Holding Company Income (FPHCI) generally consists of income such as dividends, interest, royalties, rents, annuities, gains on dispositions of property generating other type of foreign income, net gains from certain commodities transactions, net foreign currency gains, income equivalent to interest, income from notional principal contracts, payments in lieu of dividends, and income from certain personal service contracts (unless there is an exception).

---

[7] A related person with respect to a CFC is someone who controls or is controlled by the CFC, or a corporation, partnership, trust or estate which is controlled by the same person who controls the CFC.

Subpart F Income is reported on the tax returns of U.S. shareholders, whether they own the shares directly or indirectly through ownership of another foreign entity.

DORMANT CORPORATIONS

While the preparation of Form 5471 is something I would recommend being left to tax professionals. If you have a dormant corporation, you might be able to do it yourself. To be classified as a dormant corporation, a company must meet all the following criteria:

- The corporation does not own any stock or do any business with a non-dormant corporation.
- No shares of the foreign corporation were sold, exchanged, redeemed, or otherwise transferred.
- No assets of the foreign corporation were sold, exchanged, or transferred above the minimal transfer threshold (next two points).
- The corporation has accrued $5,000 or less of gross income.
- The corporation has accrued $5,000 or less of expenses.
- The corporation's assets cannot be more than $100,000.
- A dormant corporation is also not allowed to make any distributions.
- The corporation has only de minimis changes in accumulated earnings and profits or none.

Fortunately, you only need to complete the first page of Form 5471 which is pretty straightforward. You need to provide name and address, tax year, identifying number, the country under whose laws incorporated, date of incorporation, principal place of business, principal business activity, currency used, filer's category, and the percentage of the corporation's voting stock you owned during the tax year. For each dormant corporation you have, you must file a separate Form 5471. Don't forget to label the summary "Filed Pursuant to Rev. Proc. 92-70 for Dormant Foreign Corporation."

However, if you have a foreign owned corporation that does not meet the criteria of a dormant corporation, you will have to provide much more information. Form 5471 becomes more complicated and time-consuming as we move to other categories of filers. I would advise you to consult a tax professional as the penalties for failure to file or an incorrectly completed form are severe, and mistakes are very easy to make.

Now that you know what type of income will be taxed by the IRS, it's time to talk about what steps you can take to get as much relief as possible from them. You already know about the Foreign Tax Credit and the Foreign Earned Income Exclusion – but do you know everything you need to make them work in your favor? Read on to find out.

FOREIGN EARNED INCOME EXCLUSIONS (FEIE)

Do you remember my friend Laura, the self-employed English teacher in Milan, who I mentioned in the last chapter? Because Laura had been in Italy for the entire tax year and earned significantly less than the exclusion amount ($101,300 in 2016), she qualified for the Foreign Earned Income Exclusion. One also must have a "tax home" in a foreign country to qualify for the FEIE. However, anyone qualifying under either the Bona Fide Residence test or the Physical Presence test would also need to have their "tax home" in a foreign country. In Laura's case, her tax home was in Milan.

The FEIE can be claimed on either Form 2555-EZ or Form 2555. As a tax preparer, I usually use Form 2555, but if you're preparing your own return, you might enjoy the simplicity of Form 2555-EZ.

FORM 2555-EZ

To fill out the 2555-EZ[8]:

1. You must be a U.S. citizen or resident alien.
2. You must earn wages or a salary in a foreign country.
3. You must have a total foreign earned income of $101,300 or less.
4. You must file a calendar year return that covers a 12-month period.
5. You must not have self-employment income.
6. You must not have business or moving expenses.
7. You must not claim the foreign housing exclusion or deduction.

---

[8] These are the IRS instructions for Form 2555-EZ. While congress passes laws (the Internal Revenue Code), the IRS administers them, and dictates which forms can be filed to comply with the IRC.

While the 2555-EZ is an enticing option, it is not applicable to people who receive self-employed income, claimed moving expenses, or claimed the foreign housing exclusion or deduction. This becomes a problematic area for many English teachers who give private courses outside of a structured work environment, and are therefore considered "self-employed."

With my help, Laura considered claiming the foreign housing exclusion. We chose to forgo applying for the housing deduction, but there are times when it makes perfect sense for other taxpayers. The foreign housing exclusion is useful for those whose earned income exceeds the limit of $101,300. Even so, its impact is limited since the first $44.28 per day is not deductible. The Foreign Housing Exclusion is called the Foreign Housing Deduction for self-employed people, but the concept is the same.

To qualify for the Foreign Earned Income Exclusion (FEIE), one must meet either of two tests: the Bona Fide Residence Test or the Physical Presence Test.

BONA FIDE RESIDENCE TEST

This is a somewhat fancy phrase that explains Laura's situation perfectly. A bona fide resident is someone who truly, legitimately is a resident of a foreign country (don't try claiming that you're a resident in international waters, as the IRS won't be amused.). Although she was in Italy for an undetermined, potentially indefinite period, Ohio still saw her as a resident for tax purposes.

Her bona fide residency though is in Italy, where she had earned her income and was currently residing.

To use this test, one must be a bona fide resident for an uninterrupted period which includes an entire tax year. What this means is that on the first year you move abroad, as well as the last year, when you come back to the U.S., you would have to rely on the Physical Presence test instead.

- You MUST be a tax resident of a foreign country (even if the country doesn't have an income tax system, so long as they would otherwise have the authority to tax you).
- You cannot have submitted a statement to the country that you are a non-resident there (such as if you took that position to get better tax treatment there). It also means that you cannot live there as a tourist.

Every other tie to the country counts, and the Bona Fide Residence test is inherently subjective. There is an Excel file to help you determine if you are truly a bona fide resident, which you can find at tiny.cc/feie-tool. If you are unsure, I would not recommend claiming it. I advise that you use the Physical Presence test or the Foreign Tax Credit instead.

PHYSICAL PRESENCE TEST

This test is the other one used to qualify for the FEIE. Note, however, that you only need to qualify using one of the two (though having both would provide a safety net). If you are ever audited and you fail one test, you can simply provide another Form 2555 using the other test. To meet the Physical Presence Test one must spend at least 330 days in a foreign country in any 12-month period.

It needs to be an entire day. I once had a client say, "Of course I qualify. I spend all my time in Canada." This was followed by, "I just go to the U.S. once a week to buy gas." Oops.

There are, however, a couple of exceptions:

1. being in the U.S. for less than 24 hours while in transit between two foreign countries, and
2. being in international waters for less than 24 hours while in transit between two foreign countries. International waters do not count as a foreign country (hence, time spent there does not count toward the 330 days). Likewise, time spent in Cuba in violation of the embargo does not count toward the 330 days.

Because Laura was living in Italy for the entire year, she passed this test.

NON-CASH INCOME

Income that includes non-cash benefits is referred to as "non-cash income" on the instructions for Form 2555. All income is to be reported, even if it was paid in kind. If your employer provides housing, it would be included in your wages to be reported on line 7 of the 1040. This was the original reason for the foreign housing exclusion, although if your employer pays you cash and you then use that amount to pay for housing, you would also be eligible to use the foreign housing exclusion.

So, what is income then? Everything except what is otherwise excluded by the Internal Revenue Code ("Except as otherwise provided in this subtitle, gross income means all income from whatever source derived" – IRC Section 61).

Second foreign household: this refers to circumstances of civil unrest and war. Someone being a bona fide resident can temporarily relocate to a foreign country and remain a bona fide resident. It should be noted that the I.R.S. takes an extremely conservative stance on this. If you are preparing your own return, your answer will be "no" to question 8a on Form 2555.

Many expats get extremely frustrated with the U.S. tax-filing process, with its seemingly never-ending pages of questions followed by the massive crunching of numbers. I have met many of those people, worked with them, and assured them that we would be able to comply with all the tax requirements so long as we were detailed in our approach.

In Laura's case, we managed to file her taxes and her Foreign Earned Income Exclusion successfully. We also managed to receive a tax credit for the income taxes taken out by the Italian government, something that I will expand on in Chapter 5.

Now please move on to the next chapter so we can discuss deductions.

CHAPTER FOUR

DEDUCTIONS

To many taxpayers, deductions are the silver lining to their taxable income. They allow anyone to reduce the amount of income that can be taxed. You're probably already familiar with the most common examples of deductions (such as business expenses and charitable donations), but these categories get more complex when you take the whole world into account.

FORM 2555 & PASSING THE BONA FIDE RESIDENCE TEST

Part I of Form 2555 regards your personal information and residence abroad, which we've already covered in Chapter 2: Getting and Staying Tax Compliant. Therefore, I will now move on to explaining step by step how to complete the Bona Fide Residence and Physical Presence Tests to maximize the exclusion of your foreign earned income and escape double taxation.

Bona Fide Residence Test Requirements

- You are a legal resident of a foreign country or countries for a period duration of a whole tax year[9] (January 1 - December 31 for most taxpayers).

You must be either:

- A U.S. citizen, or
- A U.S. resident alien who is a citizen or national of a country with which the United States has an income treaty in effect[10].

Who is a Bona Fide Resident?

Living in a foreign country for a duration of a full tax year does not automatically make you a bona fide resident. In order to be a bona fide resident, you must meet the following requirements.

1. Establish a residence in a foreign country.
2. Reside in a foreign country or countries for an uninterrupted period of time that includes an entire tax year.
3. You cannot make a statement to the authorities of that foreign country that you are not a resident of that country and you are subject to their income tax laws as a resident.

Let's have a look what the form looks like in practice!

---

[9] "for an uninterrupted period which includes an entire tax year" IRC 911(d)(1)(A)

[10] Note that if you fall in this category, it probably means you have a green card. In this case, claiming to be a Bona Fide Resident of a foreign country could jeopardize your immigration status.

Matt moved to Thailand at the end of 2002 and is now a Thai citizen. He never gave up his U.S. citizenship, and each year he uses the bona fide residence test to exclude his foreign earned income. He earned $84,000, so we are going to exclude all his wages.

Part II	Taxpayers Qualifying Under Bona Fide Residence Test (see instructions)

10 Date bona fide residence began ▶ 12/12/2002 , and ended ▶ Continues
11 Kind of living quarters in foreign country ▶ a ☐ Purchased house   b ☒ Rented house or apartment   c ☐ Rented room
   d ☐ Quarters furnished by employer
12a Did any of your family live with you abroad during any part of the tax year? . . . . ☐ Yes ☒ No
  b If "Yes," who and for what period? ▶
13a Have you submitted a statement to the authorities of the foreign country where you claim bona fide
    residence that you are not a resident of that country? See instructions . . . . ☐ Yes ☒ No
  b Are you required to pay income tax to the country where you claim bona fide residence? See instructions . ☒ Yes ☐ No
    If you answered "Yes" to 13a and "No" to 13b, you do not qualify as a bona fide resident. Do not complete the rest of
    this part.
14 If you were present in the United States or its possessions during the tax year, complete columns (a)–(d) below. Do not
   include the income from column (d) in Part IV, but report it on Form 1040.

(a) Date arrived in U.S.	(b) Date left U.S	(c) Number of days in U.S. on business	(d) Income earned in U.S. on business (attach computation)	(a) Date arrived in U.S	(b) Date left U.S.	(c) Number of days in U.S. on business	(d) Income earned in U.S. on business (attach computation)

15a List any contractual terms or other conditions relating to the length of your employment abroad. ▶ PERMANENT WORK
    CONTRACT
  b Enter the type of visa under which you entered the foreign country. ▶ N/A THAI CITIZEN
  c Did your visa limit the length of your stay or employment in a foreign country? If "Yes," attach explanation . ☐ Yes ☒ No
  d Did you maintain a home in the United States while living abroad? . . . . ☐ Yes ☒ No
  e If "Yes," enter address of your home, whether it was rented, the names of the occupants, and their relationship
    to you. ▶

Bear in mind that the information you provide must indicate that you have established a permanent residence there. Matt has already been in Thailand for many years and has even acquired Thai citizenship. Citizenship is not required, as you can live in a foreign country and be its resident without it. In the case of an audit, the IRS will assess the validity of being a bona fide resident on a case-by-case basis. They will focus on the nature of your stay, length, and intention. If you moved abroad for an undefined period and you established a residence there, you will most likely qualify for the bona fide residence test. However, if you moved abroad for a defined period to carry out a project, you will not qualify for this test.

There's one other way to receive an exclusion of your income: the physical presence test.

To pass the Physical Presence Test, you must be present in a foreign country or countries for 330 full days out of 12 consecutive months, but the qualifying days do not have to be consecutive, and you can use any 12-month period. Both U.S. citizens and U.S. resident aliens are eligible to apply for this. This test is based entirely on the length of your stay, so you don't need to prove that you've established permanent residence anywhere. You can count the days you spent abroad for any reason. It doesn't have to be for employment purposes, and you can include your vacation time. Nevertheless, the question of what constitutes a full day arises quite often with my clients. I constantly remind them that it's the full 24 hours of a day. So, if you flew to London on June 1, at 7 a.m., your first full day will be June 2nd.

Part III Taxpayers Qualifying Under Physical Presence Test (see instructions)					
16 The physical presence test is based on the 12-month period from ▶ 01/01/2015 through ▶ 12/31/2015					
17 Enter your principal country of employment during your tax year. ▶ Thailand					
18 If you traveled abroad during the 12-month period entered on line 16, complete columns (a)–(f) below. Exclude travel between foreign countries that did not involve travel on or over international waters, or in or over the United States, for 24 hours or more. If you have no travel to report during the period, enter "Physically present in a foreign country or countries for the entire 12-month period." **Do not** include the income from column (f) below in Part IV, but report it on Form 1040.					
(a) Name of country (including U.S.)	(b) Date arrived	(c) Date left	(d) Full days present in country	(e) Number of days in U.S. on business	(f) Income earned in U.S. on business (attach computation)
Physically present in a foreign country or countries for the entire 12-month period					

If you traveled during the qualifying months, you should input the information in columns (a) – (f).

Once you complete one of the qualifying tests for the Foreign Earned Income Exclusion, you can exclude your wages on line 19 of Form 2555.

Part IV All Taxpayers

Note: Enter on lines 19 through 23 all income, including noncash income, you earned and actually or constructively received during your 2015 tax year for services you performed in a foreign country. If any of the foreign earned income received this tax year was earned in a prior tax year, or will be earned in a later tax year (such as a bonus), see the instructions. **Do not** include income from line 14, column (d), or line 18, column (f). Report amounts in U.S. dollars, using the exchange rates in effect when you actually or constructively received the income.

If you are a cash basis taxpayer, report on Form 1040 all income you received in 2015, no matter when you performed the service.

2015 Foreign Earned Income		Amount (in U.S. dollars)
19	Total wages, salaries, bonuses, commissions, etc. **19**	84,000.
20	Allowable share of income for personal services performed (see instructions):	
a	In a business (including farming) or profession **20a**	
b	In a partnership. List partnership's name and address and type of income. ▶	
	20b	

Don't forget to input the exclusion on line 21 of Form 1040.

20a	Social security benefits	**20a**		**b** Taxable amount . . .	**20b**	
21	Other income. List type and amount	Form 2555-Foreign Earned Inc/Housing Excl			**21**	-84,000.
22	Combine the amounts in the far right column for lines 7 through 21. This is your **total income** ▶				**22**	0.

It brings down your taxable income to zero.

SEVEN TYPES OF ITEMIZED DEDUCTIONS WITH SCHEDULE A

Schedule A is used to claim an itemized deduction instead of a standard deduction. It has seven categories: medical and dental expenses, taxes, interest, gifts to charities, casualty and theft losses, job expenses, and certain miscellaneous deductions. Each category has specific requirements and limitations that I will describe below.

Medical and Dental Expenses

You can deduct part of your medical expenses if they exceed 10% of your adjusted gross income (Line 38, Form 1040). If you or your spouse were born before January 2, 1951, you can deduct the part of your medical and dental expenses that exceed 7.5% of your adjusted gross income (if you're above 65), or 10% (if you are 65 or under). For example, if your adjusted gross income is $50,000 (10% × $50,000 = $ 5,000), the first $5,000 does not count.

Deductible Expenses

- Insurance premiums for medical and dental care. However, if you claim any self-employed health insurance deduction on Form 1040, Line 29, you must reduce the amount you claim on Line 1 of Schedule A by the same amount.
- Prescription medicines or insulin.
- Acupuncturists, chiropractors, dentists, eye doctors, medical doctors, occupational therapists, osteopathic doctors, physical therapists, podiatrists, psychiatrists, psychoanalysts (medical care only), and psychologists.
- Medical examinations, X-ray and laboratory services, insulin treatment, and whirlpool baths.
- Diagnostic tests (i.e. full-body scans, pregnancy tests, or blood sugar test kits).
- Nursing help.
- Hospital care.
- Programs to quit smoking.
- Weight-loss programs for a specific disease ordered by a doctor to treat specific diseases such as obesity.
- Medical treatment for drug or alcohol addiction.
- Medical aids (eyeglasses, contact lenses, hearing aids, crutches, wheelchairs, guide dogs, and the costs associated with maintaining them).

- Surgeries.
- Lodging expenses (but not meals) while away from home to receive medical care in a hospital or a medical care facility. You cannot deduct more than $50 a day, meals are not included and there is no personal pleasure, recreation or vacation while receiving the treatment.
- Ambulance service and other travel costs to get medical care. You can claim the amount you spent on fuel if you used your own car, or claim $23 per mile.
- Cost of breast pumps and other supplies that assist lactation.

Enter all your medical expenses on Line 1, Schedule A. Adjust the amount by reducing it by any payments you received from medical insurance and other related sources.

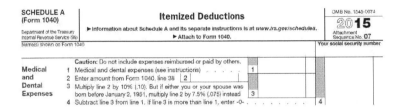

Taxes You Paid

You can elect to deduct the local and state income taxes or the local and state sales taxes, but you cannot claim both.

Income Taxes

You can deduct the state and local taxes withheld from your paycheck on the W-2, the taxes you paid during the tax year for the previous year (do not include the penalties and interest), estimated tax payments you made during the tax year and mandatory contributions.

Sales Taxes

You can deduct the state and local general sales taxes you paid during the tax year. The amount you deduct can be lower or the same as the general sales tax rate. If you paid more than the general tax rate, you can only deduct the amount you would have paid using the general tax rate. These taxes are regarding your personal property such as food, clothing, medical supplies, vehicles, etc. You cannot include the sales tax on your trade or business.

Real Estate Taxes

You can claim taxes you paid on the real estate you own for your personal use if your tax payable is assigned on a yearly basis.

Personal Property Tax

These are taxes you can claim as an expense of Schedule A if they are assigned on a yearly basis.

OTHER TAXES

If you paid any other deductible taxes, you can claim them as an expense here[11].

Bob lives in France, and he's single. He has $100,000 of general income (wages). He owes $21,071 in U.S. taxes, as all U.S. persons are taxed on their worldwide income regardless of where they reside. But he already paid $28,000 in taxes to the French government. What options does he have?

1. He can claim the Foreign Tax Credit, or
2. He can deduct the taxes paid on Schedule A.

Let's have a look what would be more beneficial for Bob.

Claiming the Foreign Tax Credit

Since the taxes he owes are less than the amount he paid to France, his U.S. tax owing will be brought down to zero. He can also use the unutilized tax credit and carry it over to future years. $28,000 - $21,071 = $6,929 remaining tax credit to use the following year!

With the Foreign Tax Deduction

Bob's taxable income is $100,000, so after computing the numbers (100,000 − 28,000 + 6,300 no standard deduction = $79,300) he will have $79,300 of adjusted gross income. The remaining U.S. tax obligation, in this case, will be $15,619 (ouch!).

---

[11] If you paid taxes to a foreign country, you can claim them here. However, it is more beneficial to use the Foreign Tax Credit.

It's not advantageous, but it is the only option if you don't have any foreign sourced income (for instance income earned on international waters)

Home Mortgage Interest

Any loan that is secured by your main home or second home, home equity loans, and refinanced mortgages fall into the category of home mortgages. Home equity loans are a type of mortgage you use to pay off your credit card bills, buy a car or pay tuition.

Any property that provides basic living facilities such as a house, condominium, mobile home, boat, etc. counts as a home for these purposes.

Limit on Home Mortgage Interest

Your deduction is limited if you took out the loan after October 13, 1987. However, if you refinanced the mortgage after this date, you can treat the new mortgage as though it had been taken out on or before October 13, 1987.

Note: If the value of the new mortgage exceeds the value of the old mortgage, the excess is treated as a mortgage taken out after the date.

If you took out the loan after October 13, 1987, and the sum of all your mortgages is $100,000 or higher, your limit is $50,000. If you took out the loan after October 13, 1987, and the sum of all your mortgages is $1,000,000 or higher, your limit is $500,000. However, these numbers only apply if you are married and filing separately from your spouse.

Computing the Numbers

The amount of your mortgage interest goes on Line 10 of Schedule A. Don't forget to enter the points reported to you on Form 1098. Any refund you received or interest you overpaid on Form 1098 should be reported on Form 1040, Line 21.

Don't reduce your mortgage interest by this amount. The points that you paid to receive your mortgage are usually on Form 1098. Nevertheless, if the points are not listed there, you can find them on your settlement statement. All the points are deductible in general, except the ones you paid for purposes other than your mortgage. If your points are not listed on Form 1098, report them on Line 12 of Schedule A.

If you or another person paid the mortgage interest, report the amount you paid on Line 11 of Schedule A.

Mortgage Insurance Premiums

A Mortgage Insurance Premium is an insurance policy paid by homeowners for FHA loans when your down payment is less than 20%. It can be deducted similar to home mortgage interest. You can deduct your qualified mortgage insurance premiums for up to three years. However, to qualify the mortgage must have been taken out after 2006. You can find your premium can on Form 1098, Box 4.

Mortgage insurance provided by the Department of Veteran Affairs and Rural Housing Services are fully deductible. You should contact your insurance provider to confirm the deductible amount of your mortgage insurance premium. The amount you can deduct is usually reduced by 10% for every $1,000, and $500 for married couples filing separately.

The deductible amount of your mortgage insurance premium is reported on Line 13.

Investment Interest

If you borrowed money for investment, the interest on it qualifies as investment interest. However, it is not deductible if the investment is allocable to passive activities or securities. You may have to file an additional Form 4952 unless all three conditions below are met:

1. Your investment income from interest and ordinary dividends (minus any qualified dividends) are higher than your investment expense.
2. There's no other deductible investment expense.
3. You have no disallowed investment interest expense from the previous year.

Enter your investment interest on Line 14 of Schedule A.

Charitable Gifts and Contributions

You can deduct any contributions and gifts you gave to charitable organizations registered with the IRS. The overwhelming majority of them are based in the U.S. Canadian charities are also eligible by using the US-Canada tax treaty. If you made contributions to any other foreign charities, you cannot claim them as expenses on your tax return. You can make contributions in many ways. They can be cash, property, out-of-pocket expenses you incurred while volunteering, and more. With a qualified charity, you can generally deduct all expenses (so long as you did not receive anything in return). For contributions that amount to $250 or more, you must provide a statement from the charity showing the amount you gave and whether you benefit from the donation or not. You must subtract any benefits from the amount you donated.

Contributions made by cash or check are reported on Line 16 of Schedule A. Other contributions, such as clothes, are reported on Line 17 at their Fair Market Value (FMV).

If you claim more than $500 of deductible charitable contribution expenses, then you must fill out and attach Form 8283. If the clothes you donated have a value of more than $500, you will have to attach a qualified appraisal as well. If you have any carryover of contributions from previous years, enter them on Line 18.

Carryover from Prior Years

Enter any carryover of contributions that you couldn't deduct from an earlier year. Remember, you can only deduct 30% or 50% of your Adjusted Gross Income as a charitable contribution, but whatever remains can be carried over for up to five years.

Gifts to Charity	16	Gifts by cash or check. If you made any gift of $250 or more, see instructions.	16	
If you made a gift and got a benefit for it, see instructions.	17	Other than by cash or check. If any gift of $250 or more, see instructions. You must attach Form 8283 if over $500	17	
	18	Carryover from prior year	18	
	19	Add lines 16 through 18		19

Casualty and Theft Losses

If you were a victim of theft or incurred a loss due to vandalism, fire, storm, car accident, or other accidents during the year, you may be able to deduct part or all of each loss. If you lost money due to insolvency or bankruptcy of a financial institution, you might be able to deduct this loss as well. If you paid for repairs to your house or appliances, enter them on Line 20. You can even deduct the cost of proving the property loss on Line 23. Complete Form 4684 and attach it to your return.

There are two requirements to claim these deductions:

1. The amount of each loss must be more than $100.
2. The total amount of all losses incurred during the year, excluding the $100 limit, is more than 10% of your adjusted gross income (Line 38, Form 1040).

| Casualty and Theft Losses | 20 | Casualty or theft loss(es). Attach Form 4684. (See instructions.) | 20 | |

Job Expenses

You can claim Schedule A expenses that exceed 2% of your adjusted gross income (Line 38, Form 1040). Unreimbursed Employee Expenses are the most common expenses claimed in this section. Your total ordinary and necessary job expenses (not reimbursed by your employer) qualify for this deduction. The amounts reported on your W-2 in Box 1 do not qualify. An ordinary expense is defined as the most common in your field of work, while a necessary expense is helpful to your business.

Enter these expenses on Line 21 of Schedule A.

Note: You must file an additional Form 2106 if:

1. You want to deduct any travel, transportation, or entertainment expenses for your job.
2. Your employer has reimbursed some of the expenses you would otherwise claim on Schedule A.

If you used your own vehicle and want to claim travel expenses incurred, you should use Form 2106-EZ.

If you don't need to file Form 2106, just list each of your expenses incurred on Line 21. If more space is required, you can attach a statement with details of your expenses and just enter the total on Line 21 with the description "See attached statement."

Generally, you can deduct all safety equipment, tools, supplies, uniforms, and protective clothing, as well as any required physical examinations, dues to professional organizations and chambers of commerce, subscriptions to professional journals, fees to employment agencies, and certain educational expenses[12].

Expenses you cannot deduct include political contributions, expenses generating tax-free income, loss of

---

[12] Exclude any educational expenses you claimed on Line 23 and tuition/fees deductible on Line 24. Certain educational expenses are subject to limitation. See *TaxTopic 513* or *Pub. 970* for details. You are eligible to take a credit instead of a deduction for certain educational expenses. See Form 8863 for details.

cash or property, expenses for meals during your working hours or overtime, travel as a form of education, fines and penalties, etc.

Tax Preparation Fees

You can deduct all the fees you paid for the preparation of your return. If you don't want to figure all this tax stuff out yourself, I encourage you to hire a professional to do it for you. Not only will you save a lot of time that you could otherwise convert into additional income, but it also lowers your taxable income and minimizes your chances of a costly error.

Enter the tax preparation fees on Line 22.

Note: If you used a credit or debit card to pay your tax owing, the convenience fee is also deductible, but it is reported on Line 23 instead.

Other Expenses

This is the field you use to deduct all the expenses incurred to generate taxable income and manage property held for generating income. You cannot claim any personal expenses here, but you can deduct legal and accounting fees, clerical help and office rent, custodial fees, investment expenses, etc.

List the expenses on Line 23. If you require more space, attach a statement to your return with a detailed list of your expenses and the amount.

Job Expenses and Certain Miscellaneous Deductions	21	Unreimbursed employee expenses—job travel, union dues, job education, etc. Attach Form 2106 or 2106-EZ if required. (See instructions.) ▶	21	
	22	Tax preparation fees	22	
	23	Other expenses—investment, safe deposit box, etc. List type and amount ▶	23	
	24	Add lines 21 through 23	24	
	25	Enter amount from Form 1040, line 38	25	
	26	Multiply line 25 by 2% (.02)	26	
	27	Subtract line 26 from line 24. If line 26 is more than line 24, enter -0-	27	

Other Miscellaneous Deductions

You can only deduct losses from gambling, casualty, theft and income producing property on Form 4684. Loss from other activities is reported on Form K-1, such as federal estate tax on income in respect of a decedent, amortizable bond premiums, ordinary loss attributable to a contingent payment debt instrument, and impairment-related work expenses[13].

Report these expenses on Line 28 of Schedule A.

If you choose to elect an itemized deduction even though it is less than the standard deduction, check the Box on Line 30.

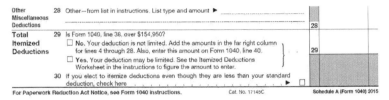

PREPARING SCHEDULE A

Preparing your taxes will be a lot easier if you have collected and stocked all your receipts in one place. Remember that you don't have to fill each line of Schedule A, but just the ones corresponding to your actual expenses.

A lot of my clients don't recognize the difference between investment income and managements fees, or

---

[13] See *Pub. 529* for details.

they forget figures such as the 2% on miscellaneous expenses or 7.5%/10% on medical expenses. Fill out the Schedule Applying the limitations for certain categories and then enter your total deductions on Form 1040.

Using standard deduction is easier than using the itemized deduction, but you need to compute the numbers to see which one will lower your taxable income. The standard deduction for 2016 for a single person was $6,300 and $12,600 for married couples filing jointly. You might be eligible to get an even higher standard deduction if you and/or your spouse are above 65 years old and/or blind.

Let's say you are 30 years old and your expenses incurred during the tax year were $2,000 of unreimbursed employee expenses, $500 of charitable contributions, and $1000 of mortgage interest. It would be better for you to use the standard deduction to lower your taxable income.

It's only a good idea to use the itemized deduction on Schedule A if it is greater than the standard deduction. A few people cannot use the standard deduction and need to use the itemized deduction regardless, such as dependents, taxpayers filing a dual-status tax return (were U.S. persons/residents for part of the year and non-resident aliens the remaining) as well as taxpayers who are nonresident aliens. Everyone else is entitled to the standard deduction, the amount for which varies based on your filing status

The 2016 amounts were:
- Single: $6,300
- Married Filing Jointly: $12,600

- Married Filing Separately: $6,300
- Head of Household: $9,300

In addition to the itemized or standard deduction, you are entitled to the personal exemption ($4,050 in 2016). Since the personal exemption is tied to a person, someone claiming dependents would also be able to claim their personal exemption for them. The IRS will check the Social Security database when processing such exemptions to avoid double claims. In the case of a name or SSN mismatch, the IRS will send an automated notice disallowing the exemption and requesting the associated tax owing, which doesn't work out well for anyone.

CHAPTER FIVE

CREDITS

Tax credits are highly sought after in this modern day of ultra-high taxation, especially by those with the highest income and therefore the most to lose. They offer ways to subtract from the total amount of tax owed after your taxable income has been fully calculated. In the case of Americans already living and paying tax in other countries, your tax credits may include what you have already paid abroad.

FORM 1116

Form 1116 is one of the most common forms I prepare for my clients. It is the form used to claim the Foreign Tax Credit (FTC), which aims to reduce the double tax burden. If you paid or accrued taxes in a foreign country, you can claim a credit for those taxes.

As you already know, your foreign sourced income is taxed by both the U.S. and the foreign country where the income was generated. If the foreign tax rate is higher than what you would be taxed at in the United States, the Foreign Tax Credit can cancel out the entirety of your tax owing.

To qualify for the credit:

1. The tax must be imposed on you.
2. You must have paid or accrued the tax.
3. The tax must be legal and actual foreign tax liability.
4. The tax must be an income tax.

Now, let's prepare Form 1116.

Jessica lives in Canada. She has $70,000 of employment income and $2,000 of income in dividends. She has paid $14,801 tax for her wages and $360 tax for the dividend income. She will need two 1116 forms, as the employment income belongs to the general category and the dividend is classified as passive category income.

Let's start with the general category 1116.

Indicate the country of residence. In our example, Jessica is a resident of Canada. You'll have to enter your gross general income (Ln 7 on 1040) in the columns illustrated above.

Ln 3, d: Your total general income.

Ln 3, e: Your total income including passive income.

Ln 3, f: The proportion of general income divided by total income. We'll use this to calculate the standard deduction attributable to general income.

Ln 3, g: Your standard deduction from your gross general income.

Next step: reporting the tax paid or accrued.

The tax you paid or accrued is entered on Ln A(n), A(r), A(s) and Ln 8.

Line A relates to income earned in Canada, which was reported in column A. If you had income from[14] other countries in columns B & C, you would report it there.

Let's figure out your tax credit now!

---

[14] Tax geeks use the term "sourced", as in "this income is sourced to Canada".

Since now we have all the numbers we need to compute the Foreign Tax Credit, we can input them in Part III of Form 1116 and calculate the credit available.

Part III	Figuring the Credit			
9	Enter the amount from line 8. These are your total foreign taxes paid or accrued for the category of income checked above Part I	9	14,801.	
10	Carryback or carryover (attach detailed computation)	10		
11	Add lines 9 and 10	11	14,801.	
12	Reduction in foreign taxes (see instructions)	12		
13	Taxes reclassified under high tax kickout (see instructions)	13		
14	Combine lines 11, 12, and 13. This is the total amount of foreign taxes available for credit	14	14,801.	
15	Enter the amount from line 7. This is your taxable income or (loss) from sources outside the United States (before adjustments) for the category of income checked above Part I (see instructions)	15	63,875.	
16	Adjustments to line 15 (see instructions)	16		
17	Combine the amounts on lines 15 and 16. This is your net foreign source taxable income. (If the result is zero or less, you have no foreign tax credit for the category of income you checked above Part I. Skip lines 18 through 22. However, if you are filing more than one Form 1116, you must complete line 20.)	17	63,875.	
18	**Individuals:** Enter the amount from Form 1040, line 41, or Form 1040NR, line 39. **Estates and trusts:** Enter your taxable income without the deduction for your exemption	18	65,700.	
	Caution: If you figured your tax using the lower rates on qualified dividends or capital gains, see instructions.			
19	Divide line 17 by line 18. If line 17 is more than line 18, enter "1"	19	0.9722	
20	**Individuals:** Enter the amounts from Form 1040, lines 44 and 46. If you are a nonresident alien, enter the amounts from Form 1040NR, lines 42 and 44. **Estates and trusts:** Enter the amount from Form 1041, Schedule G, line 1a, or the total of Form 990-T, lines 36 and 37	20	11,225.	
	Caution: If you are completing line 20 for separate category e (lump-sum distributions), see instructions.			
21	Multiply line 20 by line 19 (maximum amount of credit)	21	10,913.	
22	Enter the **smaller** of line 14 or line 21. If this is the only Form 1116 you are filing, skip lines 23 through 27 and enter this amount on line 28. Otherwise, complete the appropriate line in Part IV (see instructions) ▶	22	10,913.	
Part IV	Summary of Credits From Separate Parts III (see instructions)			
23	Credit for taxes on passive category income	23	312.	
24	Credit for taxes on general category income	24	10,913.	
25	Credit for taxes on certain income re-sourced by treaty	25		
26	Credit for taxes on lump-sum distributions	26		
27	Add lines 23 through 26	27	11,225.	
28	Enter the **smaller** of line 20 or line 27	28	11,225.	
29	Reduction of credit for international boycott operations. See instructions for line 12	29		
30	Subtract line 29 from line 28. This is your **foreign tax credit.** Enter here and on Form 1040, line 48; Form 1040NR, line 46; Form 1041, Schedule G, line 2a; or Form 990-T, line 40a ▶	30	11,225.	

Ln 19: The proportion of gross general income to the total gross income. It's used to allocate the proportion of FTC in the general category and the passive category used to offset U.S. tax owing.

Ln 20: Your U.S. tax owing.

Ln 21: The proportion of your general category foreign tax that now becomes a credit to offset your U.S. tax owing.

Ln 23: The proportion of your passive category foreign tax paid that now becomes a credit to offset the U.S. tax owing.

THE ADDITIONAL CHILD TAX CREDIT

The IRS does offer some relief and deductions for taxpayers. The Additional Child Tax Credit is a real bonus to those who have children. For each eligible child, you can receive up to a $1,000 credit on your tax owing. This is the regular Child Tax Credit. The Additional Child Tax Credit will allow you to have any remaining credit refunded. Enter it as a "payment" on your tax return.

Let's say you owe $250 in taxes. The Child Tax Credit would offset that amount, and you would then use the Additional Child Tax Credit to have the IRS send you a check for the remaining $750.

To be eligible for the Additional Child Tax Credit, the child must be your dependent, which means that he/she should be a U.S. citizen, a Canadian resident or a Mexican resident. It does not have to be your biological child. He/she can be a foster child, adopted child, dependent sibling or grandchild, so long as they live with you and meet the requirements of a dependent provided by the IRS. You can claim the Additional Child Tax Credit until the qualifying children turn 17 years old.

There are also income limitations for claiming the Additional Child Tax Credit. If you earn above a certain threshold, the amount of credit you receive goes down. Earn enough, and you'll get nothing at all. For married couples filing separately, the credit amount starts dropping at $55,000, while for a single person or the head of a household it is $75,000. For married couples filing jointly, it's $110,000. For every $1,000 of income above these numbers, the Additional Child Tax Credit goes down by $50. So, a married couple with $120,000 of income filing jointly would only be eligible for $500 of this credit.

In the next chapter, we will go over what remains of Form 1040: other taxes.

CHAPTER SIX

OTHER TAXES

We've covered the bread and butter of what goes into correctly filing your U.S. tax return. Now it's time to round out your knowledge with the periphery details that remain uncategorized by what we've covered so far.

SOCIAL SECURITY

If you're living outside the U.S., how much can you be expected to pay into U.S. Social Security? The answer, of course, depends on a few different factors – most importantly the existence of Totalization Agreements with your new country of residence. What? You don't know what a Social Security Totalization Agreement is?

The United States Government has brokered Totalization Agreements with several foreign governments – mostly in Europe – whereby U.S. citizens living in those countries would only be responsible for paying into the other country, and not the U.S. Italy was the first to enact Social Security agreements with the U.S. in 1978. Most of Europe followed suit, along with Canada, South Korea, Chile, Australia, and Japan. So, if you're paying into the

Social Security systems for any of these countries, you don't have to pay into the U.S. Social Security system.

How Social Security Changes When You Move Abroad

Social Security is a federal insurance plan providing benefits for retirees and people who are unemployed or disabled. If you live in the U.S., your employer already deducts part of your salary and pays it to the federal government to save money for your future as needed. The situation changes drastically once you move abroad.

As an American, you are obligated to pay Social Security to the U.S. government regardless of where you reside. However, some other countries offer similar programs to their residents. Thus, the United States government has established international Social Security agreements, often called "Totalization Agreements." The purpose of these agreements is to eliminate dual Social Security Taxation. Because of these agreements, if you work in Canada or Europe you won't have to worry about Social Security. Check whether your country of residence has a Social Security Totalization Agreement with the U.S.

If you live in a country without a Totalization Agreement, you may have to pay Social Security.

SELF-EMPLOYMENT TAX

People who work for themselves must pay their own version of Social Security called the "self-employment tax." It is reported on Schedule SE, flowing to line 57 of

Form 1040. Self-Employment Tax applies no matter where in the world the work was performed.

How to Calculate Self-Employment Tax

As of 2016, the Self-Employment Tax rate is 15.3%. This rate consists of two parts: 12.4% for Social Security (old-age, survivors and disability insurance) and 2.9% for Medicare (hospital insurance). The Social Security portion applies only to the first $118,500 of self-employment income, whereas the Medicare portion applies to any amount thereafter.

If you live in a country that maintains a Social Security Totalization Agreement with the United States, you do not have to pay this tax. You already contribute an equivalent in your country of residence. However, if you are a perpetual traveler who doesn't pay taxes to any particular country or the country of your residence doesn't have this agreement, you will have to pay this tax. Additionally, if your business generated a loss (or an income of less than $400), you won't owe any self-employment tax.

Avoiding Both Social Security & Self-Employment Tax

How can the Social Security burden be addressed for expats living in countries who don't share their Social Security policy with the U.S.?

Employees of all American employers must pay Social Security, no matter where they work. An American employer is defined in IRC §3121(h)(5), to include, in the case of a corporation, "a corporation organized under the laws of the United States or of any State." So, for self-employed people, the best way to ease this burden is to establish their business as a foreign corporation (i.e. a corporation established under the laws of a country other than the United States). Because there is no longer an American employer involved, the wages earned are not subject to Social Security. Be advised that if you go this route, you will have to file Form 5471 to report the interest in your foreign corporation. You will also incur the cost of maintaining the corporation abroad.

Of course, it also goes without saying that not paying into Social Security will reduce any benefit you would otherwise be entitled to at your time of retirement.

As you probably already know, the Affordable Care Act (ACA), otherwise known as "Obamacare," imposes tax penalties on American citizens without health insurance. Fortunately, anyone who qualifies for the Foreign Earned Income Exclusion is not subject to the penalties of the ACA.

SOCIAL SECURITY TOTALIZATION AGREEMENT COUNTRIES

Italy
Germany
Switzerland
Belgium
Norway
Canada
United Kingdom
Sweden
Spain
France

Portugal
Netherlands
Austria
Finland
Ireland
Luxembourg
Greece
South Korea
Chile
Australia
Japan
Denmark
Czech Republic
Poland
Slovak Republic
Hungary

If you do not live in one of these countries, you may be obligated to pay Social Security in both the U.S. and your country of residency. My friend Mark, because he currently lives in China, does not qualify for the Social Security Totalization Agreement. Although he works for an American company, because he is stationed in China he is required to follow their Social Insurance Law. It may seem unfair to pay in both countries, but he is also receiving the benefits of these taxes in both countries.

While we normally don't think of Social Security as a lot of money, dual coverage can make it much more expensive. This became an issue for Mark when his employer offered him a "tax equalization" agreement, making it so that he would earn the same "after tax" income even though two countries were taking out Social Security taxes. Because the employer agrees to cover these parts of the tax, this becomes taxable income.

Because Mark had to claim the employer's agreement, he was taxed on the money promised to him. The company covers that tax, and Mark is taxed for the increased amount promised to him by his employer. Many tax brokers know this vicious circle as a "pyramid effect, " and it can be quite costly. Thankfully, Mark came to me before the problem got out of hand. The way to avoid this involves calculating the cost of the foreign taxes, and deciding if the agreement is necessary. Although it may come with good intentions, it is often not worth the hassle of tax cycles.

Had Mark worked in a country with a Social Security Totalization Agreement with the United States, his tax situation would be quite different. Under the detached worker rule, for up to five years Mark would only have to pay these taxes to the U.S. government. Afterward, he would only have to pay the foreign government. The Totalization Agreements go further than simply providing tax relief: they ensure proper Social Security coverage at retirement. Without the agreement, the employee will still be covered in both countries, but their benefits will be determined independently. It can be frustrating to an employee who feels he/she cannot reap the benefits of the taxes enforced by both countries.

As of 2016, the United States has Totalization Agreements with only 25 countries. Although these territories are among the most common places to find U.S. expats, there are still many gaps in the system.

Taxpayers employed by a foreign corporation are not subject to Social Security tax. But what about the self-employed? While they are still able to use the FEIE, they are subject to self-employment tax as a means to pay their Social Security contribution. By incorporating a foreign corporation and receiving their income in the form of wages, they are not subject to Social Security and Medicare withholding.

Warning: be careful what you wish for. Failing to contribute to Social Security will impact your benefits at retirement. You need to decide what's more important to you before making such an impactful decision.

By now, you should understand that being an American citizen will always carry certain responsibilities and tax obligations, no matter where you live or work. These far-reaching policies are unlikely to change anytime soon, which has left many to wonder the best way to legally get out of the system. The only way to eliminate your tax obligations as an American is to renounce your U.S. citizenship officially. In the following chapter, I'll walk you through the steps that people are taking in record number to cease being an American and break up with the IRS forever.

PASSIVE FOREIGN INVESTMENT COMPANIES (PFIC)

A Passive Foreign Investment Company (PFIC) is a foreign corporation that meets one of two tests: the income test or the asset test. You will pass the income test if at least 75% of your corporation's gross income is "passive." Broadly speaking, it means that the company derives its income from investments rather than business operations. The asset test defines a company as a PFIC if at least 50% of company's assets are investments that generate or could generate passive income (such as non-interest bearing cash equivalents resulting in interest, dividends or capital gains).

While PFICs might seem like investment vehicles used exclusively by the wealthy, many taxpayers invest in foreign mutual funds, which sometimes qualify as PFICs. This can sometimes be hard to determine. They meet the income and asset tests, but it often remains unsure whether the mutual fund is a corporation. Only corporations are PFICs. To complicate the matter further, the fund must be classified as a corporation under U.S. tax principles. Foreign classifications have no bearing. For instance, Canadian mutual funds are typically trusts under Canadian law but might or might not be corporations (hence PFICs) under U.S. tax principles (the determination of which goes beyond the scope of this book)[15].

---

[15] Regs. Sec. 301.7701-3 provides that an entity is a corporation "if all members have limited liability". In 2004, various provinces

PFIC Taxation

There are three different methods to tax PFICs: excess distribution method, Qualifying Electing Fund (QEF), and the mark-to-market method. The latter two require an election. If you do not make an election, the PFIC will be taxed under the excess distribution rule (which is allocated to prior years and would be reported as another tax).

The premise of PFIC rules is that the taxpayer is investing in PFICs to defer taxation on the income. The rules are in place to create a punitive taxation regime and cancel out any benefit the taxpayer would get from the deferral.

Since most taxpayers are not aware of PFIC rules when they first invest in PFICs, many of them fail to make the necessary elections and are therefore taxed under the default regime: the excess distribution method.

The complex reporting of PFICs creates a nightmare for tax preparers, as the complicated interest and excess distribution tax are calculated separately for each block of shares with a different holding period. The exchange rate must be the exchange rate on the day of acquisition and disposition. The heavy fees and tax treatment make a fairly good investment. The form to report PFICs is

---

passed legislation guaranteeing limited liability to mutual fund investors. Indeed, in 2003, the Bank of Canada issued a report concluding that the personal liability of investors in Canadian mutual funds was possible. An entity's classification is determined when it is created. As such, there is a strong case that mutual funds created before 2004 are partnerships, and not PFICs.

Form 8621, and I would advise you to consult a tax professional when completing it. Even so, many professionals still struggle with the complicated rules that govern PFIC tax.

QEF Method

The QEF regime allows taxpayers to be taxed in the current year for the income accrued within the fund. It is only available if the mutual fund (or other PFIC) issued a PFIC Annual Information Statement. Since these documents are rarely issued, the method isn't widely used. Furthermore, you should make a QEF election when you first start investing in the PFIC.

Mark-to-Market Method

The mark-to-market regime allows taxpayers to look at the change in fair market value from year to year and report it as capital gains. Capital losses are allowed only to the extent that they cancel out prior capital gains. You cannot report losses bellow basis. Likewise, you should make an election when you first starts investing in the PFIC.

Excess Distribution Method

The excess distribution method is the most commonly used method, and it is the heaviest. It is also the default method you'll be taxed on if you have PFICs and did not make an election when you started investing. Any excess distribution or deemed excess distribution is allocated across the taxpayer's holding period. The amount is taxed at the highest marginal rate and an interest charge is added on the top of that. The interest is calculated based on the amount allocable to each year during the holding period.

The IRS defines "excess distribution" as the portion of distribution over 125% of the average distribution during the prior three-year period. For example, you receive $1,000 of distribution in 2013, 2014 and 2015. In 2016, you receive $1,500. Your taxes would be $250, according to the excess distribution under IRS Sec. 1291. $1,000 + $1,000 + $1,000 divided by 3 is just $1,000. 125% of that would be $1,250. Subtracting that from $1,500 leaves you with $250 owed.

Any capital gain resulting from the disposition of a PFIC is allocated across the holding period and taxed at the maximum marginal tax rate (39.6% as of 2016, although only 35% until 2012), and it would then have an interest charge. Over a period of a decade, one could face a tax on such capital gains of as much as 47%, regardless of what their tax bracket would otherwise be. Had it not been a PFIC, it would be a long-term capital gain taxed at 0%, 15% or 20%.

It's time to move on to our final section, and a subject that many U.S. taxpayers have reluctantly found themselves considering with greater interest than ever before: breaking up with the U.S. government for good.

CHAPTER SEVEN

HOW & WHY TO RENOUNCE U.S. CITIZENSHIP

With all the arduous requirements and liabilities that come with American citizenship, more people than ever are starting to question whether the benefits outweigh the costs. You may now be wondering yourself why you are still a citizen of the U.S. Or, if you fall into the "accidental American" category, you probably never even thought of yourself as one and want no part in their tax game. Situations like these may lead you to ask -- is there a way to end my citizenship and permanently free myself from the IRS?

The U.S. has made it costlier in recent years, but anyone can still do it. Renouncing your citizenship is not a decision which should be taken lightly. In addition to the time and money involved in the process, it's something which will forever affect how easily you can return to the United States, as well as how you are treated in other countries around the world. There is only one little-known exception: people who renounced before the age of 18 can reclaim their U.S. citizenship within the first six months after turning 18. Additionally, if you don't already have another citizenship in place before you renounce, you will end up stateless and, depending on your immigration status elsewhere, might suddenly find yourself struggling to prove your identity or move freely across international borders.

There are several ways to relinquish your U.S. citizenship. If you have taken a job with a foreign government or military, or become a citizen of another country with the intent of giving up your U.S. citizenship, you have effectively relinquished your citizenship with the United States. A few decades ago, the United States took a strong stance against dual citizenship and assumed that those who acquired a foreign citizenship did so with the intent of surrendering U.S. citizenship. The way to prove that you have relinquished U.S. citizenship is by obtaining a Certificate of Loss of Nationality (CLN). Those who indeed requested a CLN back then, or otherwise caused the Department of State to issue one, are clearly no longer U.S. citizens. There is a story of someone sending an insulting letter to Henry Kissinger, which also mentioned that he had recently become Canadian. He received a CLN in response. But nowadays, the Department of State is much, much more tolerant of dual citizenship. The onus is on the individual to convince them that he or she acquired their new citizenship with the intent of surrendering U.S. citizenship.

Obtaining a CLN can be done at a U.S. consulate either by convincing them that an expatriating act occurred with the intent of surrendering U.S. citizenship (the actions described above) or by renouncing. Renouncing is done by making an appointment at the consulate and informing them of your intent to relinquish. It is the clearest and easiest way to give up your U.S. citizenship. It is, however, only applicable from the date of that appointment. It is not retroactive, whereas a CLN obtained by having the consulate recognize an expatriating act will be backdated to the date of that event. Only then would you legally stop being a U.S. taxpayer.

If you have not filed your taxes for years (due to some non-willful reason), the Streamlined Foreign Offshore Procedures are the best way to get into compliance without having to be liable for any penalty. To become compliant under the Streamlined Foreign Offshore Procedures, you would need to file three years of income tax returns (and six years of FBAR). You could, however, elect to file more years. You would have to file five years of returns to avoid becoming a covered expatriate.

It is important to cleanly cut your ties and avoid being a covered expatriate if you don't want the IRS pursuing you for past sins. Surrendering U.S. citizenship removes your filing obligation going forward, but doesn't remove past obligations. There is also no statute of limitation on unfiled returns. Avoiding covered expatriate status also means that you can give assets to U.S. persons without making them liable for gift taxes, among other things. Once you renounce your U.S. citizenship, it's best to cut ties completely if you can. That means properly filing five years of tax returns so that the IRS will not be able to challenge these filings.

U.S. citizens will pay the same amount for a CLN whether they are acquiring it for renunciation or other forms of relinquishment. At $2,350 (as of 2016), the U.S. charges the highest expatriation fee in the world. This fee could raise at any time without reason. It was only $450 at the end of 2014. This fee is now levied to everyone relinquishing citizenship, regardless of method. It is charged on top of any Exit Tax you might have to pay as well. Still, for many, this is a small price to pay to be forever free of the sticky fingers of the IRS.

Renouncing your U.S. citizenship isn't a decision to be taken lightly, and I advise that you consult with an expert to determine if it is the ideal course of action for you (as well as the best way to tie up any loose ends before you cut the cord entirely). It's a major change in life that will affect you both personally and financially.

COVERED VS. UNCOVERED EXPATRIATES

The so-called Exit Tax refers to the fact that a covered expatriate is deemed to have sold all his or her assets at Fair Market Value on the day prior to his or her relinquishment. The associated capital gain will be taxed on his final tax return.

The Exit Tax is a capital gain transaction on Schedule D, with the sale price being the Fair Market Value on the day prior to his or her relinquishment. It will be based on the balance sheet included in Form 8854. However, the Internal Revenue Code, in its great generosity, does provide that the first $680,000 of such capital gains will not be taxed (IRC Section 877A(a)(3)(A)).

U.S. citizens who relinquish their citizenship are either "expatriates" (who are not subject to exit tax provisions) or "covered expatriates" who are subject to exit tax provisions.

So, who is a covered expatriate?

A covered expatriate is someone who fails one of the following three tests:

1. Has too much income: depending on your U.S. tax liability, $155,000 (which is indexed to inflation, per year for the last five years).

2. Has too many assets: a net worth of more than 2 million U.S. dollars (which is not indexed to inflation).

3. Fails to meet the tax compliance test: does not meet the requirements of Title 26 for each of the five years leading up to the year of relinquishment.

There are, however, two exceptions to these rules:

1. Those born with dual citizenship and are still a resident and subject to tax in their country of second residence and citizenship.

2. Those who relinquish before the age of 18 years and six months, and have not lived in the United States for at least ten years.

IRC Section 877A(g)(1)(B)(ii) states that an individual is not a covered expatriate if the following two conditions are true:

(I) the individual's relinquishment of United States citizenship occurs before such individual attains age 18.5, and

(II) the individual has been a resident of the United States (as so defined) for not more than ten taxable years before the date of relinquishment.

UNDERAGE RELINQUISHMENTS

Please be aware that intent is harder to prove for minors since the Department of State assumes that such young people have been influenced by their parents or other adults. For them, renunciations are preferable (to have more certainty that the Department of State will accept it). The Department of State will accept renunciations starting at age 16, but will likely bring up intent issues for anyone under 18. So, realistically, you have only six months immediately after turning 18 to do it. This is coupled with the fact that those under 18 can recover their citizenship if they change their mind (before turning 18.5), and the Department of State has a strong preference against doing work for nothing. They don't want to process a renunciation for someone who might request to get their citizenship back in just a couple years.

Based on all this, there are typically four categories of people who relinquish U.S. citizenship:

- (I) Born exclusively American and relinquish after the age of 18 years and six months. You will be a "covered expatriate" if you meet any one of the above three tests.
- (II) Relinquish before age 18.5 having lived less than ten years in the United States. You will be a "covered expatriate" only if you fail to certify that you have been tax compliant for the five years prior to your relinquishment.

This information is extremely important for children who are the beneficiaries of wealth (such as trusts). This is a good reason for wealthy children to surrender U.S. citizenship at a very young age. Keeping the family fortune may depend on it.

- (III) Born with dual citizenship and still living in the other country, not having lived in the U.S. for more than ten years out of the previous 15. You will be a "covered expatriate" if you fail to certify that you have been tax compliant for the five years leading up to your relinquishment.
- (IV) Born with dual citizenship, is older than 18 years and six months, and is not living in the other country at the time of relinquishment. You will be treated the same as category (I) above.

Dual citizens who intend to renounce U.S. citizenship should consider where they reside at the time they renounce. Some people go home to die. Some people go home to renounce U.S. citizenship and meet the certification requirements. If they are not met, the individual should ensure that he or she owes no U.S. income tax as they go through their unrealized gains. If there are no unrealized gains, there can be no tax base and therefore no income tax caused by "mark to market rules."

AVOIDING COVERED EXPATRIATE STATUS BEYOND THE EXIT TAX

There are two additional potential points of taxation to be aware of. The first happens when you leave the United States, but only if you have unrealized gains. The second tax point occurs when someone receives a gift from a covered expatriate (IRC Section 2801). This can occur for decades into the future, long after the date of expatriation.

It is possible for someone to have significant assets without unrealized capital gains. Both rich and poor individuals would be in the same position when they expatriate. Whether they have $1 million worth of assets or only $5,000 worth of assets, they will not have to pay any exit tax so long as they have no unrealized capital gains.

If they don't meet the certification statement (certifying that they were compliant for the prior five years), they would be covered expatriates and subject to the gift tax provision. Under IRC Section 2801, if they ever gift money to a U.S. citizen (even decades later), the recipient will have to pay a gift tax of effectively 40%. A common example is a family member who would have retained U.S. citizenship. This is why, in some families, relinquishment becomes a family affair.

YOUR FINAL TAX RETURN

After renouncing, you will have to file one final tax return and attach Form 8854.

Assuming that you didn't relinquish on January 1, your final return will be a dual-status return, meaning that it covers both a period during which you were a resident and a period during which you were a non-resident. A dual-status return takes the form of a tax return (1040 or 1040NR) with the other one being attached as a statement. The tax return is the one reflecting your status as of December 31. In our case, you were a non-resident on December 31. As such, you would prepare a tax return on Form 1040NR and attach Form 1040 after it. You would write "DUAL STATUS RETURN" at the top of Form 1040NR and "DUAL STATUS STATEMENT" at the top of Form 1040. Form 1040NR covers the period in which you were a non-resident. It would only cover U.S. sourced income (which might be zero). Form 1040 covers the period in which you were a U.S. citizen, reporting all worldwide income. It comes with all appropriate schedules and informational forms, and of course Form 8854.

WHY YOU SHOULD CONSIDER ACQUIRING A NEW PASSPORT (OR TWO)

Whether you ever plan to give up your U.S. citizenship, you should know that you always have other options. The United States is one of many countries that allows its citizens to hold multiple simultaneous passports from other nations ever since two pivotal Supreme Court rulings (1967: Afroyim v. Rusk; 1980: Vance v. Terrazas). It's getting more common now for the modern traveler to hold two or more passports obtained through entirely legal means. Unfortunately, it's also quite common to fall victim to black or gray market passport scams that promise quick results through backdoor channels and outright forgery. You don't have to resort to these scams if you understand the legal options available to you.

Having a second citizenship can facilitate travel, allowing one to get better immigration status or have a place to go back to if a worst-case scenario occurs. Being a French citizen, I can get permanent resident status anywhere in the European Union (provided I get a job there or register in their system as a self-employed person). Argentinian citizens with another citizenship fared better in 2001 during their economic depression, having the ability to resettle in another country. I expect the same to apply today to Venezuelan citizens to escape the country's current rampant hyperinflation.

HOW TO GET A SECOND PASSPORT

The best place to hold a passport depends on where you plan to travel and how hard you are willing to work to get it. If your ambitions lie in Europe, you'll probably want to get a passport from a member country of the European Union (or at least one that will let you visit the Schengen zone without a visa). South America has the Mercosur agreement, which will allow you to travel around nearly the whole continent with only your ID card and stay for extended periods of time if you are a citizen of any member country. Some former U.S.S.R. nations will give you easy access to Russia (normally very difficult for Americans) and the surrounding nations.

To become a citizen of another country legally, you are basically restricted to four options: ancestry, marriage, investment, and residence. Be wary of any shady fast talkers who claim to be able to get you a passport for any country by any other means, such as "knowing a guy" in the immigration department. It is highly likely that such a passport would be either gray market (a legal passport obtained through illegal means) or black market (a fabricated passport). They may even just take your money and run, leaving you empty handed. These horror stories are more common than anyone likes to admit. I hope that, as international lifestyles become more commonplace, this will be less of an issue. If you are suspicious of any offshore provider who makes big promises about his ability to get you another passport, feel free to contact me before proceeding as I may be able to vouch for (or dismantle) their so-called credibility.

Many countries have ancestry programs for descendants of citizens also to claim citizenship if they desire. The descent programs of Armenia, Bulgaria, Croatia, France, Ireland, Israel, Italy, Lithuania, Poland, Rwanda, Serbia, Turkey, and Ukraine extend for two or three generations, so it's worth looking into if you have a grandparent or great-grandparent from one of these places. Just be prepared to produce the documents (e.g. birth certificates) proving your lineage and take at least one trip there to apply for and/or pick up your new passport when it is ready a few months later.

Marrying a foreigner puts you on the fast track to citizenship in their country (and them on the fast track to becoming American), but the process can be different for each nation. Usually, residency is acquired first, and after a predetermined amount of time has passed you can apply for your passport.

Generally, the more developed the country, the greater the measures they will take against marriage fraud. The United States reportedly goes to great lengths to prevent illegal aliens from obtaining passports through sham (usually paid) marriages. Still, this doesn't stop many people from "helping their foreigner friends out" by entering into "on-paper" marriages with them. Due to the potential problems this can cause down the road if the validity of your marriage is ever called into question, I do not recommend that you marry someone just for their passport. However, if you happen to fall in love with someone from another country, more power to you.

For individuals of a certain net worth, economic investment opportunities exist that will either put you on the short path or instantly qualify you for citizenship. Many island nations are notorious for offering these passport opportunities at investment or donation levels ranging from six to seven figures. If you qualify, you can expect to receive your passport in just several weeks. A St. Kitts and Nevis passport allows travel to a large array of countries, including the Schengen area, but it also comes with a social stigma not otherwise associated with citizenships obtained through birth, marriage, residence, or ancestry in a world superpower. I've heard many stories from people who acquired these citizenships years ago, and still must spend several extra minutes at every border crossing as guards go through a few extra security precautions to make sure everything is legitimate. Many of them have never even heard of these nations, let alone seen a passport from one. If you are feeling thrifty and can only afford the $45,000 fee for a Comoros Islands passport, you would have much more limited travel opportunities.

Similar programs exist even in some of the most desirable parts of Europe and Latin America, such as Malta, Cyprus, and Colombia. One can also obtain a U.S. green card can also by investing $500,000 (EB-5 program). Then, one can apply for U.S. citizenship after residing there for five years. I would not recommend that such a wealthy person enter the U.S. tax system (nonimmigrant status E or L would be more appropriate), but economic citizenship is widespread indeed.

But for most people, the best way to obtain a second passport will simply be through the path of naturalization as a permanent resident. The requirements for residency vary widely from country to country. They usually involve some combination of registering a local company, investing a certain amount of money (or holding it in a local bank account), having an employment contract with a local company, and spending a certain minimum amount of time within the country each year. Some country's requirements are very easy to meet. Others are very difficult. But this is one area where having an American passport can make things a little easier for you.

American citizens are still treated with a high degree of reverence in many places that welcome foreigners. Panama is a popular choice for Americans seeking foreign residency, as they maintain a "friendly nations" visa policy with 47 countries that makes it easy to start a company and be approved for citizenship just five years later (and with minimal requirements for actually being present in the country during that time).

THE PRICE OF CITIZENSHIP[16]

Country	Investment Minimum[17]	Residence Requirements[18]	Time to Citizenship[19]
Antigua and Bermuda	$250,000	5 days in one period over 5 years	Immediate
Cyprus	€2.5 million	None (under review)	Immediate
Dominica	$100,000	None	Immediate
Grenada	$250,000	None	Immediate
Malta	€1.15 million	6 months	1 year

[16] Source: International Monetary Fund.
[17] Other forms of investment may be authorized.
[18] Extra Minimum Residence Requirements under the Immigrant Investor Program. The criteria for residence qualifying for citizenship may be different.
[19] Includes waiting period to become a permanent resident under the residency programs.

Saint Kitts and Nevis	$250,000	None	Immediate
Australia	AUD $5 million	40 days/year	5 years
Bulgaria	€500,000	None	5 years
Canada[20]	CAD $800,000	730 days over a 5-year period	3 years

THE PRICE OF RESIDENCY

Country	Investment Minimum[1]	Residence Requirements[2]	Time to Citizenship[3]
Canada - Quebec[21]	CAD $800,000	730 days over a 5-year period	3 years
France	€10 million	N.D.	5 years

[20] Program suspended since February 2014.
[21] While this is not specific to the immigrant investor program, a physical presence of 730 days over a five-year period is required to maintain permanent resident status.

Greece	€250,000	None	7 years
Hungary	€250,000	None	8 years
Ireland	€500,000	None	N.D.
Latvia	€35,000	None	10 years
New Zealand	NZD $1.5 million	146 days/year	5 years
Portugal	€500,000	7 days/year	6 years
Singapore	SGD $2.5 million	None	2 years
Spain	€500.000	None	10 years
Switzerland	CHF 250,000/year	None	12 years
United Kingdom	£1 million	185 days/year	6 years
United States	$500,000	180 days/year	7 years

CONCLUSION

We live in a rapidly changing world. The rules we were all once used to playing by no longer apply. With the recent worldwide implementation of FATCA reporting, staying under the radar while not filing the required income tax returns and FBAR is no longer a viable option. No matter how long you have laid low and kept your business to yourself, as an American citizen you are always under threat of crackdown.

Don't let panic stop you from taking the crucial step of becoming tax compliant. People like to imagine the worst. They suffer delusions of grandeur about the U.S. government keeping close tabs on their every move. Odds are, you simply aren't important enough to them (unless you are part of the ultra-wealthy or have committed serious financial crimes, such as taking active steps to hide your assets or income). It's simply a matter of preparing your returns correctly and using the resources available to keep your stress and expenses down.

You also shouldn't let this fear stop you from pursuing an international lifestyle. I know better than anyone how complex it can all seem from an outsider's perspective.

In addition to the many business and banking opportunities afforded by looking outside your home jurisdiction, it's an extremely exciting lifestyle. You will collaborate with interesting people. You will learn more about yourself and grow as a person. It's just one part of stepping into a much larger world.

You may have been reading this book in a slight state of desperation, rapidly nearing or already past the standard tax filing deadline. If that's the case, I am happy to help you file an extension. Contact me by email at owagner@1040abroad.com with the subject line "Free extension book offer." I'll get back to you to collect your SSN and address and get them filed securely. I'll gladly file your tax extension for free as thanks for reading my work.

I also created a tool to help you determine your eligibility for the Foreign Earned Income Exclusion. You can find it at tiny.cc/feie-tool. I hope that it will be useful, especially since most expats rely on the FEIE.

Finally, the only definitive way to be out of the U.S. tax system as a U.S. citizen is to be a U.S. citizen no longer. Relinquishing one's citizenship is a very personal and sometimes emotional thing to do. In my mind the most important benefit of U.S. citizenship is the ability to come back to the U.S., being able to work and stay as long as one wishes with no restriction. Additionally, if you do not have equivalent travel freedom in the form of another equally powerful citizenship, you may find yourself lamenting the loss of your previous ability to travel with little visa restriction. No matter what your situation, I do not recommend becoming stateless (i.e.

renouncing without having already acquired another citizenship). That said, I see many accidental Americans with little to no ties with the United States for whom FATCA made the decision to leave the club an easy one.

I wish you all the very best in your life of adventure outside the United States.

ABOUT 1040 ABROAD

Before obtaining my U.S. citizenship and traveling all over the world, I was born and raised in France. My experience learning the intricacies of the U.S. immigration process combined with my desire to travel freely lead me to specialize in taxes for Americans living abroad.

Americans are expatriating in greater numbers now than ever before, and this trend shows no signs of slowing. Technology is making it easier to live unconventional and location independent lifestyles. I aim to serve as a bridge between my clients and the government they are obligated to stay financially tied to.

I help Americans Abroad file their taxes and devise strategies that make sense for their lifestyle. These strategies encompass all aspects of registering an offshore business, opening a bank account abroad, and planning new residencies and citizenships.

If you are considering going abroad for even part of the year, talk to me first to discuss your options. The steps you take now will bring you greater freedom, so take the right steps from day one. Find out more by visiting www.1040abroad.com.

INDEX

58333026R10100

Made in the USA
San Bernardino, CA
27 November 2017